Why Should I Hire You?

How to Get the Job You Really Want

Why Should I Hire You?

How to Get the Job You Really Want

BY MELVIN R. THOMPSON

A HARVEST/HBJ BOOK

First Harvest/HBJ edition published September 1977

ISBN 0-15-696400-7
Library of Congress Catalog Card Number 75-822
Printed in the United States of America

Library of Congress Cataloging in Publication Data

Thompson, Melvin R.
  Why should I hire you?

  (A Harvest/HBJ book)
  Reprint of the ed. published by Venture Press, San
Diego.
  1. Applications for positions.   2. Employment
interviewing.   3. Recruiting of employes.   I. Title.
HF5383.T54   1977   650′14   75-822
ISBN 0-15-696400-7

JOVE PUBLICATIONS, INC.
(Harcourt Brace Jovanovich)
757 Third Avenue, New York, N.Y. 10017

Contents

Acknowledgment

To the unemployed, the underemployed, the misemployed, and the overemployed. To any woman or man thinking of a new job, and to anyone who should be thinking of a job. To new graduates and to seasoned job veterans I offer my appreciation, for you are my market and without you this book would be wasted.

I also acknowledge that the market for this work has been ripened by a continuing stream of garbage-laden publications put out over the years under the general classifications of job hunting, interviewing, career changing, etc.

My special thanks goes to my financial backers, most of whom are also my clients. Their faith in my product has allowed me to pick their minds as well as their wallets, and in the absence of either of the foregoing ingredients you, the reader, might never really know how to answer when you're asked,"Why should I hire you?"

I greatly appreciate the advice and assistance of Donald Merkin. Without his help this book would have been a less potent product.

Preface

Of all the many volumes published on how to get a job, or how to change careers and move ahead in business, not one mentions your name. None of them was written especially for you, and none can really tell you how to achieve these goals. At best, they can only offer guidance and information.

This book is no exception. It provides no magic buttons that will vault you out of a going-nowhere job and into a new and exciting position. But it does throw out the myths about job-hunting and quickly cuts through to the basics so that you can easily understand and apply them. It shaves the dice for you, so to speak, and tells you all you really need to know in order to be successful in the job market.

The techniques described in this book have been successfully utilized by my clients since 1970. Men and women at all levels of income and responsibility have moved ahead in their jobs and learned to control their careers by applying the simple steps contained herein. In all my years as a professional career manager I've yet to meet a working person who could call his own shots in the job market. You may never find the "perfect" job, but I encourage you to try for it. Some of my techniques will feel awkward to you when you first try them, but don't be discouraged. The best thing about this book is—it works!

M.R.T.

A Special Note to the Reader

The outside margins of most of the pages in this book are lined for your personal use. In order to take full advantage of this publication, it is suggested that you utilize this feature.

Individualize your approach to this book by making lots of notes to yourself and by circling or underscoring those sections that seem to be especially relevant to you. Treat it like a personal workbook, and be absolutely candid and realistic in your notes to yourself.

For purposes of simplification and brevity, this book contains few references to the female gender. Also, the language of this volume tends to lean toward middle- and upper-middle-income jobs. But the basics are applicable to everyone, regardless of sex, income level, or background. So when you read "he," "him," or "his," don't let it throw you. And when you read $16,500 (or some other salary) per year, simply make the appropriate conversion to suit your personal situation.

HENRY B. FOWLER

HENRIETTA B. FOWLER

INTRODUCTION

You've never had it so good, job hunter, nor have you ever had it so bad. Perhaps, my friend, you have never really had it at all.

Securing a new position is really a marketing problem. Many parallels exist between marketing yourself and marketing any commodity. Unfortunately, there are *very* few people who are qualified to market themselves. If you apply the information you are now gaining, however, *you need never again be concerned about landing "the job."*

During the course of a job interview, the interviewer will be asking, either directly or indirectly, "Why should I hire you?" He may not even be aware of this in-built question, yet that's what he's really asking. With this thought in mind, you should be aware that two major factors must almost always be resolved before you will be hired. *First*, there must be *acceptable chemistry*. In other words, the interviewer must like you. "This individual," he should say to himself, "is a person with whom I would enjoy being associated and would enjoy working eight or nine hours a day. He seems to be a person of high integrity, high intelligence, and, in short, my kind of people. He would make an excellent representative of the company, because his goals and motivations are clearly in concert with mine and with those of our firm." *Second*, the interviewer must be absolutely convinced that you will be *profitable* to his organization. He must be sure that whatever contributions you are capable of making will show up directly on the bottom line, where it counts, and fast.

Once these two major concerns have been satisfied you need not be concerned about being too old, too young, or about any of the other "negative" features you attribute to yourself. If he *wants* to hire you and has the authority to do so, he'll act affirmatively. This is, of course, an oversimplification, but remember these two points: *chemistry* and *profitability*, and in that order. The effective handling of each is vital to job-interview success.

DON'T SIT ON YOUR ASSETS

If you have little difficulty in obtaining a new position, you are probably interviewing at a level that is well below your qualifications and income potential. Any position that doesn't test your capacities is boring at best. Likewise, any position that pays you only "enough to get by on" amounts to nothing more than a means of existence. Unfortunately, very few people have enough confidence in their own talents to break out of their occupational cocoons and to accept the challenge of furthering their own professional and personal objectives. This lack of self-trust is a kind of illness that prevents an individual from developing into the person that he could be and should be. So don't let the fear of failure hold you back. If you possess talents and expertise that would be of value to an employer, you have a responsibility to yourself to head for the marketplace—the job marketplace, that is. Don't wait for the right opportunity, make it happen. Don't permit yourself to use any form of excuse, and don't procrastinate. Make your assets work hard for you.

Another type of illness that holds people back is laziness. Only a very small percentage of people in our commercial system are actually doers. A second, much larger group consists of those who observe and follow the doers. And finally there are the multitudes who sit around and wonder what the doers are doing. For this last group there is little hope. But for the second group, the observers and followers, their comfort can come from knowing that laziness is fortunately a controllable negative.

Laziness often shows itself in a person's failure to live up to his responsibilities and to keep his word. Laziness implies a lack of maturity and is usually characterized by an unwillingness to face discomfort and defeat. It can manifest itself in many forms: confusion, tardiness, excuses, mediocrity, lack of goals, lack of accomplishment, lack of aggressiveness, lack of competitiveness, and lack of interest. If you are in reasonably good physical and mental health, and if you are starting to squirm in your seat as you read this description of persons in the second group, then perhaps you should ask yourself if you are really getting the most from your life and your potential. On a scale of one to ten, how would you rank yourself in ambition? If you're short on steam you might well be in for a tough time. There is only one remedy for laziness: take positive action on your own behalf, and do it immediately. Good jobs hate lazy people. And the reverse is equally true.

Perhaps the greatest enemy of ambition is pessimism. This multi-headed beast is born out of doubt and raised in fear. Pessimism can best be conquered by success, which depends on imagination, planning, hard work, and determination. Once we force success to drive out pessimism, it then becomes a matter of *how* successful we choose to be. At that point, we must also determine just exactly how we measure success. We must define our personal priorities and measure the true value of each in relationship to our working future. We must find out exactly what it takes to make us happy in our work and commit our efforts and ambition to that end. And when you consider your own personal version of "success," remember that without a goodly portion of enjoyment and self satisfaction, your material gains aren't worth counting. Material success alone is not sufficient to motivate a person to overcome pessimism. So if proper motivation cultivates success and success overcomes pessimism, we must go back to the basics. Our values, those things in life that we consider to be most important to our individual happiness, directly control our motivation, our success . . . and our ambition.

A good example of how values and motivation affect ambition can be seen in the typical neighborhood character who gets up at a ridiculous hour, skips breakfast, dons special clothing, utilizes expensive sports equipment, drives out of his way to pick up his competition, pays a fee, then spends the next couple of hours hitting and chasing a little white ball. Ambitious? You bet. But how about the lawn in his front yard? Or the other household chores? Or voting? Or night school? And for that matter, how about the job? The career? What happened to all that ambition? Could it be that this walker of meadows, this tee tiger, this lion of the links might just reserve his ambition for something that really turns him on? Could it be that he is more interested in having fun than in working? Could it be that he would rather enjoy himself than make money, even though it will require a great deal

ILLUSTRATION 1

of effort and expense? Hopefully, the correct
answer to each of these questions is an empha-
tic yes. This hypothetical person has already
demonstrated his ambition. Even more important, he has told the world as well as himself
that he is not only willing but eager to expend
his energies when he pursues an activity that

involves placing personal enjoyment, self satisfaction, achievement, and challenge above material gain.

You can replace the golf course with the tennis court, boat, bowling alley, stamp collecting, or anything else that fits your individual situation, but I'm sure you get the message. There are really *very* few people who lack the ambition to achieve success in their work, but there are great numbers who lack the motivation. So before you decide that you simply are unable, or unwilling, to compete in the "rat race," be sure you are talking about the *right* race. Be sure you have selected the right job, the right career. Be sure you give yourself every chance to be "turned on" about your future employment.

Toot Your Horn

Ignorance is understandable and even unavoidable in many instances, but stupidity —the failure to use the physical and mental tools with which you are equipped—is inexcusable. From time to time we are all faced with losses and defeats. If we have put forth our best efforts we can usually gain a great deal of knowledge from these experiences and can later apply what we have learned to our advantage. If, on the other hand, we face defeat along with the full knowledge that we didn't really try, we are left with little room to improve our state.

No one can change you, of course, except yourself. If it is time for you to toot your own horn a little bit longer and a little bit louder but you choose not to do so, then sadly this book will be of little value to you. The job market has a low tolerance level for stupidity. And since ambition is the enemy of stupidity, you have only to get off your assets and seek out the good jobs.

You Are Unique

Imbeciles and geniuses are rare. Most of us are about equal in intelligence, and we don't need much of an advantage over our competition to be successful in the job market. I'm not referring to abilities or talents. Merely raw intelligence.

Despite the basic sameness of intelligence, however, no one person in the world is exactly like any one else. This uniqueness, if you are willing to take advantage of it, can make the difference between failure and success. You know your unique characteristics, your weaknesses and your strengths, better than anyone else. Learn to capitalize on your strengths and to neutralize, or at least minimize, your weaknesses. You are equipped with enough ambition to act but you must first choose to utilize it—the outcome is *entirely up to you.* Remember that the primary advantage you have over your competitors is your uniqueness—those special assets that set you apart from the rest of the world.

Decision Time

Any decision we face in life should be executed by weighing two major factors: the probable risk against the probable result. And so it is with job hunting. You alone are in a position to measure the risks, effort, time, and expenses of a job search against the probable results of a new and better way to spend your working hours. And only you can make the decision to change or stay put. Of course some have acquired new positions through chance or by accident, but because luck is a pretty fickle ally, this form of career Russian roulette is best left to those who can fully afford to lose. And don't delay making career judgments. Life is more exciting today than ever before. Right now there are more opportunities and more challenges than ever before. It's fine to learn from yesterday and to plan for tomorrow, but living is for today. I suppose just about everyone has had their share of the "If only I had started five years ago"s, but we mustn't allow ourselves to dwell upon any past lack of action. If we are to go ahead with our careers we must decide, then act. Needless delay of decisions or actions can not only cause added difficulties in the achievement of goals, but can oftentimes literally destroy the opportunity itself.

A Slight Advantage

This society of ours is not really made up of the "haves" and the "have-nots" so much as it is of the "doers" and the "non-doers." Once you have made the decision to act, this book will become a close and helpful friend. And like any valuable friendship, you take from it in direct proportion to the amount that you give. Read and remember and reread. Then apply. Seek and secure the proper career objectives. Make this book a highly personal property. Make notes, underscore the parts that you consider to be especially important to *you*. If you feel so inclined, tear out pages and do whatever else you choose. Just be sure you accept it for exactly what it is—a slight advantage. A slight advantage that your competition doesn't have. And that's all you need.

THIS LITTLE PIGGY WENT TO MARKET: COMPETITION

The job market in any given area is, in part, a reflection of that particular area's economy —the factor that determines the number of jobs available versus the number of people available to fill them. But finding the job you want can be a formidable task, regardless of the state of the economy. In a "good" market, plenty of jobs are available and competition appears to be low. This appearance is deceptive, however, because competition is always intense for the really good job—that is, the one at the highest level for your qualifications. Perhaps now is the time for upward mobility, for promotion or maybe for that long-overdue change you have been toying with for so many years. A "tight" job market goes hand in hand with reduced profits, and reduced profits cause turnover in many positions. It really matters very little whether the job market is "good" or "tight" at any given time, since job changes continue, and the demand for talented people to fill good jobs never ceases. Your competition in the job market is exceedingly keen, however, and thousands of highly qualified people can compete effectively for your present position or for the position you may want to seek. For whatever solace it may offer, though, remember that your competition probably knows no more about securing a new position than you do. A *slight* advantage will give you a major edge on your competition *if* you are willing to put that advantage to work for you. Most people are ignorant of the job market and don't know the first thing about marketing themselves. Most job seekers are still living in the horse-and-buggy days of submitting resumes, chasing help-wanted ads, sending out broadcast letters, and interviewing with employment agencies or personnel departments. What a waste!

Indeed, you have a great deal of competition but, for the most part, your competitors are ill-informed about this business of landing the right job. Accordingly, the "slight advantage" you will have over your competitors should make you look pretty good in comparison —even in spite of yourself.

THE GENERAL JOB MARKET

The current statistical breakdown of unemployed persons looks something like this:

- Five percent elderly persons.
- Ten percent who have quit their jobs.
- Fifteen percent who are *not* heads of households.
- Thirty percent who are students, previously unemployed women, and other first-time job seekers.
- Forty percent who have been fired or laid off.

These figures give you a rough idea of the *unemployed* segment of your competition. But don't get hung up on numbers, since they don't in any way affect your *needs*. And besides, the really stiff competition lies within the *employed* market, since about twenty-five percent of the entire job market change jobs each year. (Think about that one.)

Eighteen percent of all currently employed males are actively seeking a new position; thirty-four percent are "inactively" looking; and another thirty-one percent would "consider" a job change. This leaves only seventeen percent of the employed males who indicate that they would *not* change jobs. And of that percentage there are many who feel forced to remain in their present jobs for one reason or another. Only *three percent* are actually doing a job they really like. This surprising statistic may in part reflect the fact that thirty-nine percent of all employees with academic degrees are *not* working in their chosen fields.

Additionally, the work force is younger than ever, and most fields emphasize youth and

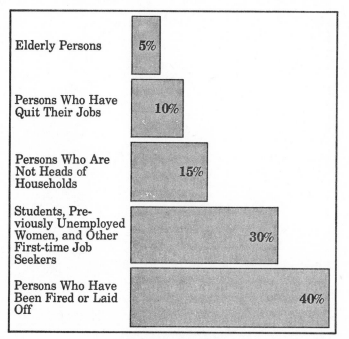

ILLUSTRATION 2

vigor. The hard chargers are replacing individuals with experience and maturity, those who heretofore were so much in demand. And as the average age of the work force decreases, job-hopping becomes more and more common and acceptable. In fact, if properly handled, job-hopping may very well prove to be a major career-growth advantage.

Of executives and technical experts planning job changes, a whopping forty percent have been in their present spots for only two years or less, twenty-six percent for three to five years, and fourteen percent for six to ten

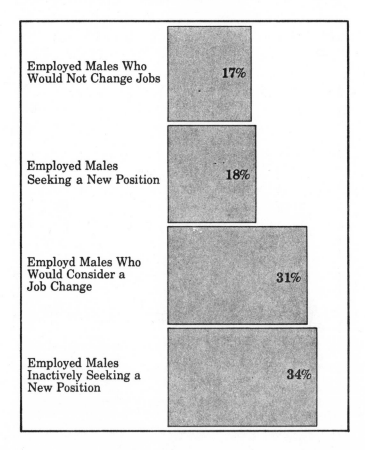

Employed Males Who
Would Not Change Jobs   17%

Employed Males
Seeking a New Position   18%

Employd Males Who
Would Consider a
Job Change   31%

Employed Males
Inactively Seeking a
New Position   34%

years. In these times, the corporate policy of hiring new employees and letting them prove themselves before paying close attention to their progress can be self-defeating in terms of retaining needed talent.

After salary and responsibility, geographic location is the third most important consideration in making a job change, which indicates that people are genuinely concerned about how and where they want to live. Although the hub of the job market has traditionally been centered in or around the big cities, today more and more people are willing to forego an exceedingly attractive position in the city for the comfort and security of a rural area. Much like retailers, who moved away from the metropolitan areas to accommodate buyers, employers who recognize this trend have headed for the hills to attract talented employees.

All in all, the job market can best be described as an ever-changing set of conditions, which, though highly unpredictable, are directly tied to the lifestyles of the work force. People outgrow jobs and companies; jobs and companies outgrow people. Thus the job market is probably the most changing of all markets, moving with the inevitable law of supply and demand. In the job market, however, it is easier to create a demand (job) than in most other markets. Any company, large or small, has a bundle of problems—and therein lies the need or "demand." The job seeker has only to define his particular market and its demands, then set about to satisfy those demands with his personal time and talent. There will never be a poor job market, only poor job seekers. And here's an interesting observation based on years of working with job changers at all levels of the market: The higher one's previous level of employment, the more assistance he usually needs in making a change—a fact that most of these people don't recognize.

It isn't at all surprising that the very young and inexperienced job seekers usually do so well when they receive proper counseling. The fact is, they have fewer bad habits to break than their older, more "seasoned" competition.

The extreme variance in job-getting abilities among people is a tremendously important factor in judging the job market. The market must be measured not only in terms of the number of available positions (and positions that can be made available) compared to the number of available people, but it must also be gauged in terms of people best qualified to get the jobs. In other words, you must decide how you stack up in the job market using several approaches:

1. Your ability, in relationship to your competition, to perform the responsibilities required by existing and available positions.
2. Your ability, in relation to your competition, to perform the responsibilities required by positions that will soon become available.
3. Your ability, in relation to your competition, to perform the responsibilities required by positions that you or others can soon create.
4. Your ability, in relation to your competition, to get job offers.

Of the above four approaches, the last is by far the most important and the most deciding.

Regardless of the availability of good jobs and your qualifications to handle them, you're apt to have tough sledding if you don't know how to get interviews and job offers. Conversely, you'll probably do well, even in a tight market, if you are an expert at "marketing" yourself.

_____

_____

_____

_____

_____

_____

_____

_____

_____

_____

_____

_____

_____

_____

_____

_____

_____

_____

I.
GOALS:
Where Now Brown Cow?

LEAVING THE NEST

"Company loyalty" might better be described as "inflexibility," or an exaggerated need for security. The employee who claims he "can't afford to leave" his job may well be suffering from a self-inflicted overdose of fear, and probably wouldn't give serious consideration to a new opportunity even if it fell in his lap. But if he does finally decide to make a move and makes his intentions known, he might learn that any loyalties that existed between him and his company were pretty thin and one-sided. If this sounds anti-employer, it's because it was intended that way.

Careers can be effectively managed, but remember that your career is *your* sole responsibility and any move you make is entirely up to you. If you don't do it, who will? If you dodge this responsibility and allow your employer to control your fate by passively accepting any job he offers you or by accepting his orders without question, then you might as well let him determine your eating and dressing habits as well. For after all you are only a prisoner of his will. Don't waste time by staying in a job too long and permitting your employer or the calendar to control your progress. Stay mobile, stay flexible, stay alert, and stay visible. Exposure breeds opportunity.

TWO KINDS OF GOALS

If you have decided to seek a new position, you are ready to set some goals. You have two kinds of goals to deal with, short term and long term. Every short-term goal should represent a step toward a long-term goal. If it doesn't, you are not recognizing the shortest distance between two career points. And if you don't have some goals to aim for, it's unlikely that you'll be going very far, very fast.

It's terribly important for you to remain alert to opportunities, but just be certain that you zero in on the *right* opportunity. A lack of goals can get you into trouble. Unless you have made an effort to define your goals, there is no way for you to recognize the right opportunities. And if you seize upon the wrong opportunity, you will most likely have to move backward at some point in time and redefine your career path.

Long-term Goals

Let's talk first about long-term goals, for if you don't know where you are going, you probably don't know how to get there. Your initial step is to work out a goal calendar (See Illustration 4). Make your goals realistic but not easy. Define your long-term objectives clearly and concisely *in writing*, and keep your calendar in a prominent and conspicuous spot as a constant reminder. (Don't be limited by the sample illustration. No two people will complete this chart in exactly the same way.)

When you put your objectives in writing, be sure to include your titles, responsibilities, authority, salary, and anything else that seems important. Take yourself on a hypothetical journey through your entire career, step by step, from this day forward, considering your needs and your desires. Of necessity, your charting will be governed by your present feelings but should not be unduly influenced by the current job market or by your abilities as you now perceive them. Don't be timid. And

Age	Goals	Company Profile
65	*SENIOR VICE-PRESIDENT.* Major management responsibility. Salary open. Stock options.	
60	*CORPORATE VICE-PRESIDENT* or *DIVISION MANAGER.* Management and profit responsibilities. Salary open. Stock options.	65
55	*CORPORATE VICE-PRESIDENT.* Small to medium company. Report to president on special projects. Salary $24,000-$30,000.	60 / 55
50	*CORPORATE CONTROLLER.* Complete fiscal responsibility. Report to president. Salary $20,000-$25,000. Car and expense account.	50
45	*CORPORATE CONTROLLER.* Complete fiscal responsibility. Report to president. Salary $20,000-$25,000. Car and expense account.	45
40	*ACCOUNTING SUPERVISOR* or *DEPARTMENT HEAD.* Complete accounting responsibility. Small department. Salary $16,000-$19,000.	40 / 35
35	*ASSISTANT MANAGER, ACCOUNTING DEPARTMENT.* Minor supervisorial chores. Department of not less than 16 people. Salary $15,000-$17,000.	
30	*SENIOR ACCOUNTING CLERK.* Small to medium department. Salary $11,500-$14,000.	30
25	*ACCOUNTING CLERK.* Small department. Salary $8,500-$9,000.	25

ILLUSTRATION 4

don't be afraid to use your imagination or to
fantasize about your future, for regardless of
where you now stand on the career ladder, it's
never too late to start moving upward. Your
present and past positions are relatively unimportant. Above all, don't compare yourself
with anyone else, and don't let your charting
be guided by the advice of a friend. Make this a
highly personal project, setting forth a series
of difficult but achievable goals. And don't
chart in a hurry. This procedure requires logical, mature thinking. Although you will most
likely change or modify your goals through the
years, they are extremely important to you in
determining your immediate course of action.

Also take into consideration the things you
are capable of learning in the future, and don't
forget the opportunities that will be created by
the ever-changing job market. List the long-
term objectives you feel you can achieve, given
the right set of circumstances and conditions.
If you let your past track record get in the way,
it might become an anchor that you have no
business dragging along with you, so concentrate on the future. Your future.

Illustration 4 shows the work of a rather
ambitious charter, and not everyone will want
to shoot this high. But regardless of what your
goals are, be sure to define them and to *put
them in writing*. Your long-term goals represent your destinations and your timetable for
getting there, and the effort you spend in
charting your goals at the outset of your job
search can pay great dividends down the road.

Short-term Goals

Now let's discuss short-term, immediate goals,
keeping in mind that each short-term objec-

Unless you really have fun doing whatever it is you choose to do for a living, there is little likelihood that you will ever be successful doing it.

tive should represent a vital step toward achieving a long-term goal.

At this point you are ready to set some basic job parameters (See Illustration 5). Make up a list of everything you *want* in your next job. These considerations may change later—and that's fine, as long as you hold on to your basic values, the things that are really important in your life. Your family structure or your financial requirements may change, for example. You may even decide at a later date to completely overhaul these guidelines. The point is that we are talking here about *immediate* considerations, not about rules that you have to live with forever. List everything that you feel is important and reasonable. And keep working at it until you can begin to aim for your career objectives with a rifle rather than a shotgun.

A COMPANY PROFILE

After you have outlined your job parameters, you will have what amounts to a company profile, including a number of clearly defined short-term considerations. Once you have formulated a general idea of the sort of company you want to work for, you are ready to become much more specific. Thus your next

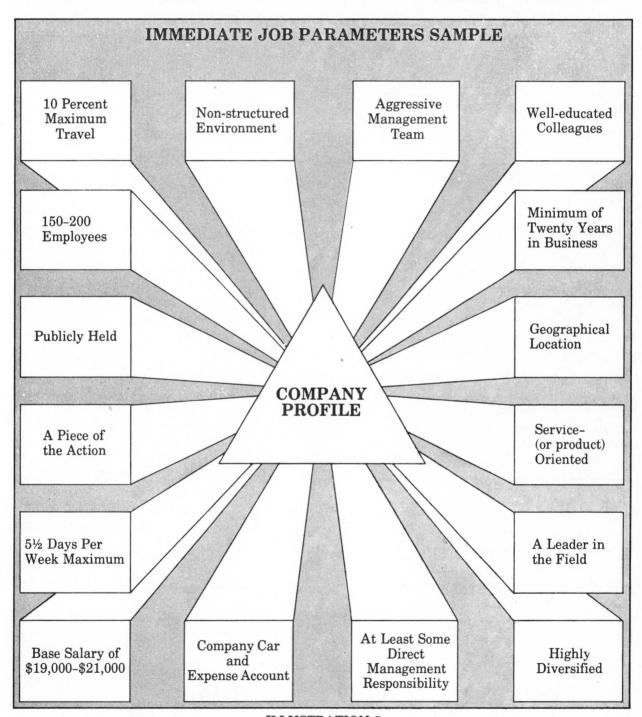

IMMEDIATE JOB PARAMETERS SAMPLE

10 Percent Maximum Travel

Non-structured Environment

Aggressive Management Team

Well-educated Colleagues

150–200 Employees

Minimum of Twenty Years in Business

Publicly Held

Geographical Location

COMPANY PROFILE

A Piece of the Action

Service- (or product) Oriented

5½ Days Per Week Maximum

A Leader in the Field

Base Salary of $19,000–$21,000

Company Car and Expense Account

At Least Some Direct Management Responsibility

Highly Diversified

ILLUSTRATION 5

_____

_____

_____

_____

_____

_____

_____

_____

_____

_____

_____

_____

_____

_____

_____

_____

_____

step is to take a broad look at the possible choices of products or services that are available to you. This step is particularly vital to those who are contemplating a career change.

Consider every type of company and activity you can think of that seems to contain something of personal interest to you. Take a good look at each alternative before you start weeding them out. Most libraries offer numerous publications listing products, services, and job descriptions; be sure to make lots of notes as you review them. You might also go through the index of your telephone directory as it can provide a great source of ideas. Take into special consideration all of your personal likes and dislikes—the types of people you like to associate with, the clothes you like to wear on the job, the degree of public exposure you prefer, the amount of travel, authority, and responsibility you desire, the services and products that appeal most to you, the size of the company, and so forth. Consider every product or service that lights even the smallest fire in you. Keep an open mind, and whenever you find yourself interested in a subject or category, make a note of it. If you approach this exploratory task with imagination, you will end up with a list of fifty or perhaps even a hundred different products or services which, for whatever reason, you find of interest.

A New Sort of Six-Pack

The next step is a bit more taxing. You must now methodically and objectively go through your list of services or products, keeping only those that genuinely appeal to you. Limit your list to a maximum of six choices. If you do it correctly, you will find that this process can become quite time-consuming, but don't be intimidated. Your efforts will be well-rewarded later. Be sure to consider each of the factors you defined earlier in making your company profile, and remember to use a healthy blend of optimism and realism.

After you have reduced your areas of interest (product or service) to six, you must then select six companies in each category that seem to coincide best with your needs. List them by category and in order of your personal preference. The thirty-six firms on this list will later serve as your targets for interviews and job offers. Prepare a form using Illustration 6 as your model. In the future you can use this interview grid as a working guide for investigation and interviewing. Once you have actually begun your interviews, you should continually update the form by deleting any firms that have been eliminated during the interviewing process and by inserting your next choice (in order of preference) at the bottom of your list. In other words, the company appearing in block 1-1 should always be your first choice, and the company appearing in block 6-6 should always be your last. Detailed information, such as research data and notes from your interviews, should be kept in a separate, alphabetized file.

When you are considering the types of companies best suited for the achievement of your goals, be sure to do your homework. Select only those companies offering services or products that are on the way up. Stay with the growth industries. Avoid both "ground-floor" opportunities (those that have yet to prove their future) and opportunities in an industry that is about ready to peak. Get in on the first or second floor. The ground floor is too close to the basement, and the floor next to the top

INTERVIEW GRID (List by order of preference)						
	Name of Company					
	1	2	3	4	5	6
1 Service or Product Position Desired						
2 Service or Product Position Desired						
3 Service or Product Position Desired						
4 Service or Product Position Desired						
5 Service or Product Position Desired						
6 Service or Product Position Desired						

ILLUSTRATION 6

	Approximate Job Title	Approximate Job Description
First Choice	Vice-president Marketing	Corporate officer, manages 15–20 people, market planning and strategy, gets input from customer service and controller—reports to president.
Second Choice	Assistant to the President	General trouble-shooter crosses corporate lines of authority, puts out all types of fires, acts as extension of president—reports to president.
Third Choice	Sales Manager	Recruits, trains, and leads salesmen. Sets quotas, hires and fires, initiates new techniques, increases sales—reports to Vice-president marketing.
Fourth Choice	Field Representative	Works without close supervision to sell company service or product. High degree of travel—exceeds quotas—reports to sales manager.

ILLUSTRATION 7

leaves little room for upward mobility. Bet only on known winners. You might even select a product or service that you like, but can't decide for sure how you really fit in. In such cases, you might want to wait until the first interview with a prospective employer to define the exact position for which you would like to be considered.

A first interview with a firm is, in many cases, mainly designed to obtain information and, in the event the situation warrants it, to arrange for a second interview. For the most part, however, you should already have a pretty good idea of how you could best serve a company *before* your interview with it. Illustration 7 will help to guide you in this procedure.

II.
EVALUATION:
Time to
Take Inventory

"People can be divided into three groups: those who make things happen, those who watch things happen, and those who wonder what happened."
John W. Newbern

_____
_____
_____
_____
_____
_____
_____
_____
_____
_____
_____
_____
_____
_____
_____
_____

WHAT ARE YOU SELLING?

Self-evaluation is always difficult and can often be unpleasant. It requires complete honesty and objectivity, a combination that's sometimes tough to come by. But if you are to sell yourself in the job market, you must first determine exactly what you are selling—and,

We all live in the grip of attitude

The big question is — is it positive or negative?

ILLUSTRATION 8

equally important, what you are not selling. Like any product, you possess many features, some of which are attractive to your market and some of which are not. As with any marketing problem, you must take full advantage of your marketable qualities, while preventing your unmarketable features from killing the sale.

Before getting into the details of your pros and cons, let's discuss the two most important factors in self-marketing, *attitude and motivation*. Fortunately for you, these are factors over which you have complete control.

What Makes Henry Run? And Why?

Personal attitude is grossly underrated as a factor in obtaining a job and advancing within a firm. Like the individual who is content with an "adequate" or "comfortable" compensation package, a job applicant with a "satisfactory" attitude seldom stands out in a crowd. Attitude helps to develop rapport or "chemistry" during interviews, and without the right chemistry it is unlikely that employers will beat a path to your door. A poor attitude magnifies weaknesses and negatives. A good attitude brings out strong points and successes. You probably can't change your personality but you *can* change your attitude. What's more, you can make the kinds of changes that will give you the greatest advantage in seeking a new job. Be positive in everything you do, and your chances for success will be increased immeasurably. Besides, a positive approach is a lot more fun.

TEST YOUR ATTITUDE
A good way to begin (if you have the stomach

"There is very little difference in people, but that little difference makes a big difference. The little difference is attitude. The big difference is whether it is positive or negative."

C. Stone

---

for it) is to prepare a brief questionnaire about your attitude, and then ask eight or ten people who are reasonably well-acquainted with you to give some honest *written* responses. Choose people who, in your judgment, are strong enough not to be swayed by your friendship and whose opinions you respect. Here are some questions you might want to include (you can add others if you wish):

1. Do I always do my best?
2. Do I always look at the bright side of things?
3. Am I friendly and cooperative?
4. Do I do more than my share?
5. Do I appear to be confident?
6. Am I believable?
7. Do people see me as a leader?
8. Do I appear to be trustworthy?
9. Do I appear to be intelligent?
10. Do I dress tastefully?
11. Am I well-mannered?
12. Am I well-poised?
13. Am I tactful?

14. Do I appear to be mature?
15. Do I attend to details?
16. Am I personable?
17. Which of my outward weaknesses do you consider might have a negative effect on my success during an interview?
18. Am I ambitious?
19. Am I open-minded?
20. Do I follow through?
21. Am I optimistic?

When you draw up the questionnaire, be sure to leave plenty of room for remarks after each question. It takes a bit of courage for your friends to level with you, so impress upon them the importance of an honest and full response. When you analyze the completed questionnaires, you will get a rough idea of how other people see you. Pick out your weak and strong areas, then improve your attitude by correcting the weaknesses and emphasizing the strengths. You'll be surprised how quickly you will notice the results.

If you have a particularly stubborn weakness, find someone who is strong in that specific area and ask him for advice. Chances are that a thirty-minute conversation with him will put you on the road toward correction. Also, you might want to read any of a number of good books dealing with attitude and motivation. Most of them are worth reading—but don't get carried away or become overly inspired.

Changing your negative traits takes time and effort. But it must be done if you are to fulfill your ambitions in the job market. And once you have made the change, you must pay constant attention to it or you will probably slide back into your old ways. Stay with it.

TIME AND EFFORT INVENTORY				
Week Number	Accomplishment	Approximate Hours Spent	Approximate Hours Required	Lost Hours
1				
2				
3				
4				
Totals				

ILLUSTRATION 9

Attitude makes all the difference in the world. It's also contagious, and can be a powerful tool in influencing other people—either negatively or positively.

Time for a Tune-up?

I'm not sure that I agree with the old adage "he who hesitates is lost," but I do believe that "he who hesitates will usually continue to hesitate" and will probably end up giving only a small part of himself to mankind.

Few people live life to its fullest. Few of us ever really test our capacities or develop our talents to their optimum. If you are running on only half of your cylinders, you are already ahead of your competitors, and if you are running on one-third power, you are probably on about an equal par with them.

You can test the validity of these statements by taking an informal time-and-effort inventory, using actual accomplishments as indicators of your productivity. At the end of each work week, list your ten major accomplishments for that week. Opposite each accomplishment make a note of the amount of time *required* to complete it—not necessarily the amount of time it took *you*, but the minimum amount of time you realistically think it *should* have taken. Keep your weekly tabulations for four weeks. Could you have done more? You bet your sweet W-2 you could have. Try about four-hundred percent. Chances are that your own honest scrutiny will demonstrate that the same achievements that took four weeks could have been comfortably handled during a one-week period.

There are lots of trees in this immense orchard of opportunity in which we all live. So shake each tree as hard as you can for maximum options. If you happen to uproot a given tree, simply go on to the next, and you'll soon discover that there is literally no end to this vast and exciting orchard of possibilities.

WHO'S ON FIRST?

Can you do your boss's job? Forget for a moment about your experience and credentials and ask yourself honestly, "Can I really *do* his job?" If something were to happen to him, could you step in and, after a short briefing period, take over his assignments and do them at least as well as he is doing them now? If your answer is yes, then why does he have the job and not you? Because he has been with the company longer? Because he had some lucky breaks? A better academic background? Whatever your answer, it is probably only an excuse. The point is that your boss could just as well be your competitor, and if taking over his job would be the only way for you to advance, yet all the signal lights are red, then you had better either get out your green paint or change companies. And if you can't do your boss's job, you might consider a reassessment of your qualifications in terms of your goals.

If you think you are worth more than you are being paid but you are unwilling or unable to be competitive in a competitive market, unwilling to face the possibility of frustration and defeat, unwilling to gamble for fear of losing, unwilling to change a situation in which you are stymied by your own weaknesses and by your unnecessary and mistaken concern for your fellow human beings, then you might just as well calm your feeling of frustration by carrying your six-pack to the television set, where you can be content with what you have and worry no more about your professional growth. On the other hand, if you really want to contribute to your company, to your fellow humans, and to yourself and your family, and if you are really willing to put out, then push yourself to the highest level of your capabilities and achievement. Within the limits of honesty and fairness, let nothing stand in your way— especially yourself.

Do It Yourself

You alone are responsible for your career —which means that *you* can control it. But since your career is your sole responsibility, it is up to *you* to plan, engineer, and secure your objectives. If you take this responsibility seriously and do everything within your power to achieve and manage a rewarding career, you will benefit greatly. But if you make only a partial effort or no effort at all, don't expect a greater return than what you have put in. There is absolutely no room for neglect and no time for procrastination. And planning alone is not enough. You must cross the bridge after you build it. So act—and do it now.

YOU ARE A BUSINESS

Securing a new position is much like going into business for yourself. *You* are the product or service. *You* are the President, Controller, and Head of Marketing all rolled into one. *You* have all the problems and benefits of a self-contained business. This concept will permit you to approach your situation from the same objective standpoint that you approach problems in your normal business environment, and the sooner you learn to deal with yourself in this manner the better.

_____

_____

_____

_____

_____

_____

_____

_____

_____

_____

_____

_____

_____

_____

_____

_____

_____

_____

Your abilities are the exclusive properties that will help you market yourself, and they will make a more impressive list than you might think. For example, if you are a salesman your skills may include door-opening techniques, customer relations, proposals, sales, closing techniques, consumer psychology, advertising, contracts, and contract negotiations. If you are an electronics engineer your skills may include circuit design, drawing control, customer relations, systems, buying proposals, contracts, and so forth. Whatever your occupation, don't restrict yourself. Don't live within the strict confines of your past positions, and don't permit your job history to categorize you. Most people restrict their job future to fit their past, and in so doing they become their own worst enemy. This sort of danger is vividly illustrated by highly qualified, retiring military people who think they must find someone to start a war in order to become fully employed.

Take Inventory

Your transferable talents make up a major part of the inventory that you, as a self-contained business, will be offering for sale. Take a very close look at yourself. Review your background, your abilities, your limitations, and, most of all, your accomplishments. Enumerate any and all achievements that you can justifiably take credit for. _Write them down_, and then convert them in terms of dollars, percentages, time required, savings, and so forth. In other words, spell them out in such a way that they are readily identifiable as "transferable skills" and marketable items.

No matter what titles and responsibilities you have held, you have been directly or indirectly involved in the fiscal success or failure of your employer. If you were the number-four man in a department of five, then you helped number three to help number two to help number one to show a profit or to create a savings. And if your department was instrumental in helping the company as a whole, so much the better. Make sure to state clearly the end result of each effort, the time involved, and how you accomplished it. It's a good idea to

_____

_____

_____

_____

_____

TRANSFERABLE SKILLS SAMPLE

Transferable Skill	Accomplishment	Result
1. Sales	Took over failing sales route and initiated automatic "call back" system. Also developed and implemented an informative products newsletter.	Increased sales by 37% to $191,700 in just twelve months.
2. Employee Relations	Faced with low employee morale and high employee turnover, I established uniform company policies and procedures and defined them in handbook form. I then commenced monthly employee/management meetings in order to keep personnel informed and to air complaints and suggestions.	Annual reduction in employee turnover from 37% to 16%. Approximate annual savings to company of $78,000 in hiring and training expense.
3. M		

ILLUSTRATION 10

	SELF EVALUATION SAMPLE	
	Positives (Sell this column)	**Negatives** (Neutralize this column)
1	People Oriented	Short on Experience
2	Progressive Salary History	Low Recent Salary
3	Well-organized	Poor Eye Contact
4	Well-dressed	Stutter
5	Poised and Personable	Sporadic Track Record
6	Good Vocabulary	Job Hopper
7	Well-traveled	Poor Public Speaker
8	Good Motivator	Divorced
9	Excellent Academic Background	Limited Management Exposure
10	Outstanding Profit Record	Underweight
11	Innovative and Imaginative	Lack of Direct Profit Responsibility
12	Hard Worker	Too Old
13	Effective Negotiator	Non-profit Background
14	Excellent Financial Planner	Procrastinator
15	Speaks Two Foreign Languages	
16	Expert in S.E.C. Rules	
17	Corporate Tax Specialist	

ILLUSTRATION 11

think in terms of P.A.R. — *Problem-Action-Results*. Use this formula as a guide when you are defining your past accomplishments.

Here's an example: "Out of eighteen separate profit centers in our national system, my department was next to the last in new accounts. I initiated a program which allowed a forty-eight hour maximum time for replacing defective parts and by setting a self-imposed quota of twelve 'new-prospect calls' per month for each field representative, gross sales went up $93,540 with no increase in operating costs. Profits increased $39,470 and my department moved up to second place in new accounts. And all in just seven months."

Problem—Action—Results

Build a strong case for yourself in terms of P.A.R., and come up with as many accomplishments as possible. Don't misrepresent, but don't be bashful either. And by all means be precise and to the point. You can elaborate later during an interview.

Now list your strengths, or positive attributes (See Illustration 11). If you are an "excellent" manager of people don't refer to yourself as merely "good." If you know you have an analytical mind, note it. If you think you are a good negotiator, financial planner, troubleshooter, and administrator, put them all down. Since you will be selling all these strengths later, you need to know beforehand what you are selling and why your prospective employer should buy it.

Now take a look at your weaknesses, or negative attributes. As distasteful as it may be, define them, put them in writing, and then learn how to deal with—and hopefully eliminate—them. The objective isn't to dwell on negatives but to neutralize them so that they won't later get in the way. If you are unsuited for a particular role or function, admit it, make a note of it, then forget it, and don't incorporate it into your game plan. The best way to deal with a negative factor is to face it head on. Don't make an issue of it, but give it enough careful thought so that you can keep it from influencing your positive areas.

Break a Leg

Physical handicaps are among the simplest negatives to overcome. Few people confuse a physical imperfection with lack of talent. The strength and courage that a person uses in overcoming a physical impairment are the very same tools that might be needed to excel in a new position.

Countless people of talent and courage have thumbed their noses at their physical misfortunes and run ahead of the pack. Consider Elizabeth Browning, Franklin D. Roosevelt, Jill Kinmont, George Wallace, Ray Charles. The list could be expanded indefinitely, but the point is that all these people had the will and discipline to control their careers, in spite of their handicaps. If you don't have a physical handicap you no doubt have a social handicap, or an educational handicap, or some other kind of handicap. One thing is certain: When you finally interview for your ideal job, you will either be the wrong height, weight, sex, or age, or you'll be rejected because of your religion, politics, or race; perhaps you'll limp on your left leg when the interviewer was looking for someone who limps on his right. Or maybe all of the above. Think about it. There is no such thing as the "perfect candidate" for any job, and most handicaps become negatives during an interview only because the interviewee permits it to happen. So if you are a few years older or younger than you wish you were, if you don't have a degree in a given discipline, or if you are light on experience, don't let it stop you. We are all imperfect beings. Remember: *capitalize on your positives and neutralize your negatives.* Take advantage of your strengths, my friend, before your competition takes advantage of your weaknesses. Even if you don't feel a need to win, develop a hate for losing. Losers don't sleep well.

III.
PLANNING:
Prime the Pump

_____
_____
_____
_____
_____
_____
_____
_____
_____
_____
_____
_____
_____
_____
_____
_____
_____
_____

MOUNT UP AND MOVE OUT

Now that you have set your short-term and long-term goals, and have completed your self-evaluation inventory, you are ready to attack the market. So let's take a look at some of the basic tools you'll need.

1. *Telephone Answering Service.* Having an answering service will help you avoid calls that might come at awkward times. Returning rather than receiving a phone call gives you the advantage of being fully prepared to talk on your own terms and at your chosen time. The expense is minimal, since the service is only temporary, and the privacy and businesslike approach that it affords are well worth the investment.
2. *Business Cards.* These should be plain and tasteful, printed on white stock. List only your full name, your address, and the answering-service phone number.
3. *Letterhead and Envelopes.* Nothing fancy, but in keeping with your business cards.
4. *Resume.* (More on this subject later.)
5. *Typewriter or temporary secretarial service.* Don't cut corners or do a shoddy job. Keep copies of your correspondence. Set up a separate file for each company you contact, and keep the files current. If your spouse or a friend has good secretarial skills, you might not have to hire a helper. You won't need a lot of help, but you do need the best. If you are shooting for a high-paying position, you should consider putting together a formal proposal to submit to your target

companies, or at least a well-thought-out presentation of your views and ideas. You might work up a four- or five-page summary of the company, its business, and its potential based upon the information you have gathered—and don't forget to include yourself in the presentation; remember that's the reason for preparing it in the first place. If you put it together properly you can use it very effectively *after the second interview*. At that point you should understand the company's basic problems well enough to outline in fairly general language your ideas about how they might be resolved. But don't make your proposal so detailed that you end up giving away some of your desirability. Make it just interesting enough to whet the interviewer's appetite and to demonstrate that you have done more than an average amount of homework. This sort of presentation can frequently replace a company's requirement for your resume and helps to avoid standing in line with your competition.

6. *Office* or at least a quiet, private place to work. A bedroom is fine.

7. *Calendar Book*. Keep a detailed record of your appointments and what was discussed. You might need it later for income-tax purposes and for job-searching follow-up.

8. *Card File*. Use 5″ x 8″ cards filed alphabetically by company name. Keep a record of people's names and titles, conversations, interviews, and personal observations so that you may refer to them later. This system should supplement a *company* research file (see

---

below). Both files should be updated regularly and kept permanently. They are easy to maintain and could result in unforeseen opportunities at some future date.

9. *Company Research File.* Any information (no matter how insignificant it may seem) that deals with your target companies—their employees, their ownership, their products, their services—must literally become your business. You will never know enough about these things—but then neither will the people who interview you. No one person ever has the final word in his field. Someone always comes along with a better way, and if you are that someone, you can bet it won't happen by accident. Illustration 12 gives you a few of the many sources of information that are available to you. But gathering information is only a part of your task. You must also digest it, understand it, and put it to work for you.

One of your best sources of information is the people who interview you—but first use all other sources you can find. Former employees of your target companies are excellent sources too. Especially those who have held jobs similar to the one you have in mind. Make it a point to find these people and talk with them, preferably in person. You'll be surprised by the amount of valuable information they can provide. Present employees are also good sources, but be careful not to go too far in questioning secretaries and assistants (touchy territory). In some cases, after the first interview you can simply

ADDITIONAL SOURCES
OF INFORMATION

Newspaper Libraries (Clippings)

Public Libraries

School Libraries

Standard and Poor

Who's Who?

Securities Brokers

Chambers of Commerce

Professional and Trade Associations

Commercial and Industrial Directories

Advertising and Public Relations Firms

Management Consultants

Utility Companies

Banks

Attorneys

Governmental Agencies

Trade Papers and Journals

Dunn and Bradstreet Million
    Dollar Directory

Dunn and Bradstreet Middle
    Market Directory

Moody's Manuals

Fortune Magazine 500 Listing

Thomas Register of American
    Manufacturers

Funk and Scott Index

PAIS Bulletin

ILLUSTRATION 12

_____
_____
_____
_____
_____
_____
_____
_____
_____
_____
_____
_____
_____
_____
_____
_____
_____
_____
_____

request permission to talk with other key people. And don't overlook competitors. You can probably gain valuable knowledge (and perhaps more interviews) by making personal calls on employees of competing firms and even on employees of firms that utilize the target company's services or products.

Find out everything you can about who is doing what to whom in a given field. Check prices, products, services, warranties. Check past, present, and future markets. Talk with the heads of top competing firms. Ask them what makes them successful. Talk with the heads of the less successful competing firms. Find out what makes them less successful. Look for the weak areas and the strong areas, and then apply the information you have gleaned to the company with which you are to interview.

Put yourself in the position of an individual who is about to make a major investment in your target company. Make a list of the factors that have directly contributed to the success of your competitors, then make a list of their soft spots. Put it in writing. When you talk with employees of a company that is strong in one particular area, find out how they got there. At some point their strong area was probably a weak area. Find out how they changed things and apply the information to the company with which you are to invest (interview) if it has a similar weak area. Conversely, you might find that the competition's major weak areas were at one time strong areas. Do your best to determine what caused them to go downhill, and see if perhaps some parallels exist in the company with which you are to interview. By now you should begin to realize how very important your research efforts are. Don't hesitate to call on bankers, attorneys, accountants, suppliers, and anyone else who has had dealings with your target companies or their customers or competitors. Probe deeply. If you talk with enough informed people, you will be able to establish an accurate pattern of a company's negative and positive features as well as to educate yourself about the field in the process.

10. *Proper Clothes.* You have only one chance to make a good first impression, so wear your "Monday best." If you are unsure about how to dress for an interview make some inquiries—perhaps of a secretary you know—and wear whatever is appropriate for the occasion. Probably as many job offers are lost through inept and improper dress as through improper interviewing. Some of the more common mistakes are listed below:

MALE
- Saggy socks (especially with a little flesh showing)
- Short-sleeve shirts
- Gaudy jewelry
- Dirty fingernails, hair, or glasses
- Unpolished shoes
- Bright colors
- Overly "mod" appearance

Packaging
Your
Product

ILLUSTRATION 13

_____

_____

_____

_____

_____

_____

_____

_____

_____

_____

_____

_____

_____

_____

_____

_____

_____

- Extreme hair style
- Ill-fitting or outdated apparel

FEMALE
- Overly "mod" appearance
- Extreme hair style
- Short mini-skirts
- Low-cut blouses
- Gaudy jewelry
- Too much make-up
- Too much perfume or cologne
- Uncomplimentary design or color combination

Take a look at the top-level executives of prestigious companies. Leaf through Fortune magazine, and you'll begin to get the picture. Why do most stock brokers look alike? Because they are selling a business, just as you are, and they must instill in their customers a feeling of confidence, trust, and believability. How to dress is really a matter of good taste and common sense, but, regardless of your personal styles, appearance must always be near the top of your planning priorities. If you feel that you will lose some of your individuality by dressing the part, think again. You'll have plenty of time to dress as you like *after* you get the new job. Most employers stay clear of job candidates with radical behaviors, and that includes dressing habits.

Most of us find it difficult to take a truly objective look at ourselves. It would be helpful to spend fifteen or twenty minutes before a videotape camera conducting a mock interview with a friend or associate. If you have never been through this experience, you may be surprised to see how you appear to other people. You might use the facilities of a local university or television station.

11. *Professional Assistance (Optional Tools)*
    A. *CAREER-MANAGEMENT FIRMS*
    Perhaps the most effective step you can take to advance your career is to obtain the services of a professional career-management firm, not to be confused with employment agencies or recruiters. The good firms will be selective in accepting clients and will not guarantee you a new position. The not-so-good firms usually employ the stereotypical suede-shoe-type "counselors" and use high-pressure sales tactics. Before you make such a move, visit all qualified firms in your area, and select the one that seems best suited to handle your particular situation. Be sure to select a firm that will stay with you *after* you get the new job and not one that merely "assists" you into a new position and then moves on to the next client. Charges for such services may range from $300 to $8,000. Be leery of companies that charge a variable fee. In such cases the company representative with whom you first talk usually establishes the fee, and all too often the amount is based primarily on your ability to pay.

    A truly professional career-management firm will not arrange interviews for you nor will it "place" you in a position. It should be

_____

_____

_____

_____

_____

_____

_____

_____

_____

_____

_____

_____

_____

_____

_____

able, however, to provide you with a great deal of assistance, including complete office services: secretarial help, business cards, telephones, duplicating equipment, postage, research information, resumes, business proposals, and other tools you may need. Additionally, it should be exceedingly close to the job market both in your area of the country and in your chosen field. It should be staffed by competent counselors with successful backgrounds, and they should not be limited in the amount of "one-to-one" counseling time they can spend with you. Your relationship with a career-management firm should be akin to that of an attorney or an accountant with his client. It should be a private and professional relationship, with trust and confidence on both sides. Be sure that the firm you choose will be working strictly on your behalf and in your best interests. (It should not receive fees from any source as a result of your acceptance of a new position.) Ask to meet the members of the staff who will be working directly with you, then talk with them long enough to determine whether they are your kind of people.

Joining hands with a career-management firm is sometimes regarded by the unknowing as the lazy person's way of getting a job. In reality quite the opposite is true, since such firms can never take your place in an interview nor can they accept or reject a job offer on your behalf. Despite the fact that you may be able to go a lot faster with professional help, you are still the one who is really responsible for your career.

The better career managers will insist on interviewing you or screening you to get a good picture of your objectives *before* they commit their company to work with you. Career managers don't stay in business by producing failures, and if your ambitions are not realistic they want to know it in advance *before* they become involved with you in a client-counselor relationship.

Career-management firms are usually aware of a number of job situations, but be wary of firms that make a major issue out of their "connections." Such connections, even if they do exist, probably can't offer you precisely what you are looking for anyway, but just for kicks let's say that you are handed a position on a silver platter. Big deal. That's simply a matter of getting you a *job*. If you are serious about a career, a new job is only the first step in the responsibility of a career-management firm.

B. *HEADHUNTERS*

Executive recruiters (headhunters) will ordinarily prove to be of little or no help to you in obtaining a new position. If they are good, they are hired by a company to find a person for a particular job, and their fees and expenses are paid by their client company. Their loyalty, therefore, is to that company, not to the job seeker. In other words, they don't work for you, they work for their

—————————————
—————————————
—————————————
—————————————
—————————————
—————————————
—————————————
—————————————
—————————————
—————————————
—————————————
—————————————
—————————————
—————————————
—————————————
—————————————
—————————————

company clients, and most of them could care less about you and your next job unless you just happen to fit an exact slot—and that possibility is *highly* unlikely. Professional recruiting firms usually charge a fee of twenty-five percent of the first annual compensation package and confine their activities to jobs with salaries in excess of $20,000 per year. For example, the fee charged by a recruiter for filling a position paying $28,000 per year would be around $7,000. In many states (such as California at $20,000) the minimum salary for positions filled by firms other than employment agencies is established by state law, and headhunters are not licensed or regulated as employment agencies.

Many executive-recruiting firms employ specialists who work mostly in one particular field. If you do choose to visit a headhunting firm, first determine which specialist, if any, is best qualified to handle your special talents and direct your selling efforts. Good luck! You'll need it!

Executive-search firms (recruiters or headhunters) receive countless unsolicited resumes. These resumes are quickly screened for any negative aspects, such as age, salary background, experience, sex, education, and so forth. A resume that survives this initial screening process is then evaluated in terms of precise company requirements. The searcher knows exactly what he is after, and unless your resume is an exact fit, he won't waste five seconds on it. So if you're thinking about sending your written life story to a headhunter, my advice to you can be summed up in one word—*don't.*

Remember that search firms do not work for *you.* They work for their client companies. Even if they grant you an interview after you submit an unsolicited resume, the searcher may very well be gathering information for his own use with no intention of seriously considering you as a candidate to fill a position. And in the unlikely event that you obtain a position in this manner you still will have had absolutely no say in putting the position together. You can say yes or no, and that's about all. A recruiter's responsibility is to negotiate *against you* and *for his client.* If he can latch on to a $20,000 person for $15,000, he will be in good stead with his client company. So be sure you know who your friends are—and who they are not.

C. EMPLOYMENT AGENCIES

This segment of the "people" business is the most controversial. It's unfortunate that employment agencies, as a group, have such a poor reputation since they should be in an ideal position to provide a valuable service to the job seekers.

Some employment agencies, of course, are staffed by competent people and are dedicated to serving their clients in a professional manner, but such firms are in the minority. The better agencies almost always charge the employer, not the job candidate, for their services.

Unlike executive-recruiting firms, they are permitted to handle jobs at any salary level, although they tend to stay away from the high-paying positions. Don't expect such agencies to look out for your interests. If they are paid by their company clients, they have no obligation to individual applicants. They, too, receive stacks of resumes and screen them to look for a potential marriage. They are in the body business and don't ordinarily get paid by their client company until after they fill a job order. Even so, they won't waste their time with you unless you are a marketable product. They will look at you through the eyes of their client, and if you don't fit the precise requirements for a particular job order, you might as well hang it up.

Private recruiting firms and employment agencies fill only about five percent of all jobs. State agencies fill only about ten percent. The other eighty-five percent of the jobs are in the "hidden" market. In other words, almost all job openings are never made known to state agencies, employment agencies, or search firms. Here's another point. When you talk to an employment agency about a job order to be filled, you can almost bet that any number of competing agencies are trying to fill that same order. The employment agency that requires a retainer and an exclusive contract from its company client before accepting a job order is rare indeed—and well worth dealing with.

If you consider the extremely high fees paid to agencies and recruiting firms, you'll probably conclude that your chances to negotiate a higher salary are much better in cases where an employer is not required to pay a "placement" fee. And you're quite correct.

Be especially careful in dealing with an employment agency where the applicant pays the fee. I have never advised anyone to pay for a job, and I can't think of any set of conditions that might alter my thinking.

IV.
PREPARATION:
Always Be
Over-Prepared

THE FUN BEGINS

Can you use the telephone effectively? Can you write effective letters? Can you prepare a good resume? No? Well, don't panic, my friend, few people can. Let's cover some "how to's" and see if we can at least keep you out of trouble.

Using the Telephone

When you talk with someone in person you can see and be seen, hear and be heard. The telephone simply eliminates sight for both you and the person you are talking with. Neither of you is at a disadvantage—unless, of course, one is less effective than the other in conversation.

Your telephone conversation should flow as naturally and evenly as it would if you were sitting across the table from the other person. Here are some basic guidelines:

- Be brief—not abrupt, but to the point. Limit most calls to three minutes. Pretend to yourself that each call is *very* long distance and expensive.
- Never permit yourself to be interviewed by telephone. Don't take unnecessary risks in matters that you can handle best in person. You should use it primarily to set up or to confirm appointments.
- Be yourself, especially when you call "cold," without an invitation of some kind. Probably the worst that can happen is that your party will hang up on you, and even then you probably haven't lost anything. *Relax.*
- Don't take lots of notes during a phone conversation. If you do you won't hear all you should hear, or think as rapidly and clearly as you might. Concentrate on the conversation.

- Don't address the party on a first-name basis without an invitation. After the other person calls you "Henry," you may call him "Mel," but not before.

- End the conversation on a definitive note, such as "I'll see you Thursday at four" or "I'll call you tomorrow morning between ten and eleven." Maintain *control* so that the next move can always be initiated by you. If your party makes no objection, it is safe to assume that he has agreed.

- Be sure you have privacy. Background noises or interruptions have no place in good phone habits. If you call from a pay phone, charge the call to your home number so that the operator won't break in if your time expires.

- Make notes of pertinent information *after the call*, and update your files accordingly.

Talking on Paper: Correspondence

A letter is nothing more than written conversation. There are definite guidelines that govern the overall appearance of a business letter, but the words should be your own. Most letter writers try to duplicate the words of other writers and end up making the same mistakes.

"Talk" your words onto paper. Can you imagine yourself actually saying to someone in a conversation, "Yours of even date?" Of course not, so don't use it in a letter. Instead, write "Your letter of last Thursday" or "Your note regarding our interview."

First, determine the purpose of your letter, then get right to the point. As with telephone conversations, be warm, natural, and courteous, but don't get carried away. Most letters should be no more than three short paragraphs. The style should be your own, and your letters should represent a direct extension of your personality. Formality and informality will vary according to circumstances, and only you can judge the appropriate amount of each. Here are some samples for various occasions.

FOLLOW-UP AFTER THE FIRST INTERVIEW:

Dear Mel:

I've come up with some ways to reduce your accounts-receivable problems, and since I want to hear more about your long-term plans for the company, let's try to kill a couple of birds at once.

I'll call your secretary Friday morning to arrange a time.

Regards,

Henry

OR

Dear Mr. Thompson:

I enjoyed our talk and certainly appreciate your time. I know how busy you are—I had no idea we had used up a full hour.

Have a nice vacation. I'll call your secretary while you're away to set a time for us to pick up where we left off.

Best regards,

Henry Fowler

SETTING UP THE FIRST INTERVIEW—WHEN HE WON'T RETURN YOUR CALL:

Dear Mr. Thompson:

Since I haven't been able to reach you by phone, I'll try a note. You have 8,760 hours each year, and so have I. I'd like to trade half of one of my hours for half of one of yours, and I'll do my best to see that you come out ahead.

I'll call your secretary on Thursday and if you have no objection, I'll ask her to put me on your calendar.

Very truly yours,

Henry Fowler

TO A COMPANY PRESIDENT PRIOR TO SETTING UP THE FIRST INTERVIEW FOR A SALES MANAGER POSITION:

Dear Mr. Thompson:

I know quite a bit about your industry and your product. However, I would like to know more about you and your company.

I understand that you might have a few unemployed salesmen on your payroll. If this is true, I think I can help you trade them for some producers.

I'll call your secretary on Monday to set a convenient time to see you.

Very truly yours,

Henry Fowler

_____
_____
_____
_____
_____
_____
_____
_____
_____
_____
_____
_____
_____
_____
_____
_____
_____
_____

PRIOR TO SETTING UP THE FIRST INTERVIEW:

Dear Mr. Thompson:

Bill Gaff suggested that I talk with you about your need for a Head Cashier.

You folks have an outstanding public image, and I would certainly like to meet you in person.

I'll call your secretary on Thursday to set up a time.

Sincerely,

Henry Fowler

OR

Dear Mr. Thompson:

Yesterday's article in the Wall Street Journal must have rung a familiar chord with your competitors, for I'm sure that the steel shortage has taken its toll with them as well. The cancellation of your particular order, however, coming as it did just prior to your annual meeting, can make for a most unpleasant afternoon with your shareholders.

I eat that sort of problem for breakfast. I'm a corporate fireman with the right equipment to back me up. My professional existence is literally committed to making my boss look good—all the time. And I have some ideas that I want to try on you.

I'll call your secretary Thursday afternoon, and if you will authorize her to set an appointment sometime next week, we can have at it for a half-hour.

Regards,

Henry Fowler

PRIOR TO SETTING UP THE SECOND INTERVIEW:

Dear Mel:

The more I learn about your product and how it benefits your customers, the more enthusiastic I become. You've given me some interesting highlights, and now I'm ready for the nitty gritty.

I'll call your secretary on Wednesday to see if we can set a time for Thursday.

Very truly yours,

Henry

Get the idea? Reduce your talk to writing. Here are a few pointers:

- Mark all letters and envelopes "Personal and Confidential."
- Mail only originals signed in ink.
- If you are writing on a first-name basis, sign only your first name above your typed full name.
- Check carefully for errors and smudges.
- Enclose stamped, self-addressed envelopes when appropriate.
- Use letters extensively to pave the way for "cold calls" and first interviews.
- Send thank-you or follow-up letters after interviews as appropriate.
- Maintain your sense of humor, but don't be cute.
- Be definitive when you end your letters. Don't leave things hanging.
- Be sure the recipient of your letters knows that he or she must take some sort of action

or else assume a position of agreement.

- Do not attach a resume (except under *very* unusual circumstances).
- Do not use the word "interview." Take it out of your vocabulary. Replace it with "appointment" or "meeting" or some other appropriate word.
- Don't sound pleading, apologetic, condescending, or weak.
- Be different. Stand out. Don't sound sterile or routine.
- If you are writing on a first-name basis, scribble (legibly) a one-line statement across the bottom of your letter such as "Mel, let's shoot for Friday morning. H."
- Don't use "Sir" (and don't use it in an interview either).
- Don't keep repeating the recipient's name in the letter.
- Use full and accurate company names, personal names, and titles. If you aren't sure, call and ask a secretary.

Preparing a Resume

By all means prepare a complete resume. *But do it primarily for your own use and not as a means of obtaining interviews or job offers.* Working up a resume forces you to define the product you are putting on the market —yourself.

Properly done, your resume should present at least a partial list of your accomplishments. It can help you to translate your work experience into talents that are transferable and potentially profitable to prospective employers. Just don't make the mistake of using your resume to get interviews or job offers. Its main

WHY SHOULD I HIRE YOU? 73

purpose is to help you to define your past accomplishments so that you can re-package them for a prospective employer.

You will also want to prepare one or more short resumes, which, *if absolutely necessary*, you can provide on request for potential target companies. In such cases, try to tailor your resume to a particular position, using an abbreviated version of your detailed resume.

The best you should expect from your resume is that it won't get in your way, that it won't turn off the reader. Most resumes go onto a stack with a hundred others. Then a clerk or secretary is instructed to screen out the undesirables (anyone over forty or under thirty, anyone without nine years experience in a given field, or anyone whose initials spell a dirty word ends up on the "you've-had-it" stack). Even if your resume survives this preliminary screening and leads you to an interview or even a job offer, you haven't really had a thing to say about creating and selecting your job. You haven't had *control* of your career. Again your choices are very simple: either say, "yes, I'll take it," or "no, but thank you for considering me anyway."

I've never seen a good resume. It's just that some are less offensive than others. Even so, here are a few resume pointers (also see Illustrations 14, 15, and 16):

PHOTOGRAPHS. *Never* include a photograph. The employer may not like blonds or glasses or the color of your skin. Anytime you reveal such things before getting an interview, you are asking for trouble. And it's not legal for an employer to require it. A company that is really on its toes will probably avoid inter-

```
------------------------------------------------------------------
HENRY B. FOWLER/1230 LIVE OAK LANE/LOS ANGELES, CALIF. 93210/(213) 555-4506
------------------------------------------------------------------
```

GENERAL BACKGROUND

Marketing manager. Expertise in product design and development. Market research, advertising, and development/training of sales forces. Experienced in sales to commercial and military in the U.S. and abroad. All facets of business operations.

Innovator -- Quickly analyze difficult problems and develop solutions.

Motivator -- Inspire loyalty and respect in others, thereby helping them achieve highest levels of performance.

CAREER HIGHLIGHTS

1971 - present   Electronics Components Manufacturer
                      Los Angeles, California

                      As Vice President of Marketing for this newly formed
                      company, faced the necessity of immediate and profitable
                      sales. Developed a marketing plan, selected and trained
                      a sales force, and sold several select accounts.
                      Results: Company sales rose from 1.8 million to 3 million
                      in a 12-month period with a bottom-line increase of 32%.

1965 - 1971   ABC Manufacturing Company
                      Chicago, Illinois

1967 - 1971   West Coast Regional Sales Manager. Substantially in-
                      creased sales each year. Consistently developed and
                      trained superior salesmen, many of whom were promoted
                      to positions of high responsibility.
1965 - 1967   Sales Engineer. Responsibility for developing new ac-
                      counts on West Coast, a previously untapped market. Des-
                      pite severe competition, I determined market potential,
                      established contacts, and successfully sold my company's
                      products. Results: Obtained first-year sales of over
                      $1,500,000, and firmly established new sales territory.
                      Won Salesman-of-the-Year award, and was promoted to Re-
                      gional Sales Manager.

EDUCATION   B.S., Engineering
                      University of Southern California

                      M.B.A.
                      U.C.L.A.

PERSONAL   Married, three children
                      Excellent health
```

ILLUSTRATION 14
```

HENRY B. FOWLER
8260 Adams Avenue
Boston, Massachusetts
(617) 302-4321

GENERAL

All phases of business operations, including sales, marketing, production and general management. Effective problem solver. Ability to mold a sick company into a highly profitable operation.

Examples:

1)   For young company analyzed market, provided necessary equipment and procedures, hired and trained personnel, expanded facilities, and developed company into largest supplier in its field. Results: Doubled sales in two years. Advanced from Salesman to Sales Manager to Executive Vice President in three years.

2)   For an established company developed marketing and quality control procedures, and provided market penetration. Results: In one year, brought company from $1 million annual sales to $2.2 million.

WORK BIOGRAPHY

3 years (present)   Assistant Operations Manager
                       ABC Manufacturing Company
                       Boston, Massachusetts

2 years   Assistant to V-P Operations
                       XYZ Company
                       Hartford, Connecticut

4 1/2 years   Operations Administration Aide
                       Engineering Representative
                       Adams Company
                       West Hartford, Connecticut

EDUCATION

B.S.M.E., M.I.T.

PERSONAL

Married, 1 child
Excellent health

ILLUSTRATION 15

HENRY B. FOWLER
1234 Oak Street
Chicago, Illinois
(312) 555-1618

SUMMARY OF QUALIFICATIONS

Top financial executive. Broad knowledge of business organization, engineering, finance, production, and sales.

Superior skill in financial and other reports to meet the needs of managers at all levels; work and communicate with sales, engineering, and production personnel, and motivate them to attain company goals.

TYPICAL ACCOMPLISHMENTS

ABC Company
Chicago, Illinois

A newly acquired, major division was virtually out of control as a result of too many employees and poor supervision. I was hired to help turn the operation around.
***Streamlined controller's functions, retrained personnel, reorganized procedures.
Results: Reduction of staff by 16, direct savings of over $200,000 in salaries; sharply improved operations and profits.
***Established basic operational/financial forecast system with input from all levels of management.
Results: Usable, accurate and timely information available at all levels. For the first time, the Chief Executive received information necessary to operate the division profitably.
Overall Results: The division is now a major profit center.

XYZ Corporation
Minneapolis,
  Minnesota

Guided the financial management of this small manufacturing company through a period of rapid growth and acquisition by a large conglomerate.
***Established complete accounting system.
***Conducted feasibility study for computer use, selected equipment, and implemented installation and applications.
***Developed operational/financial forecasting system to provide accurate management information and controls.
Results: Highly efficient operations. Of twenty companies acquired by the conglomerate in a two-year period, I was the only Controller not replaced by the Home Office.

ILLUSTRATION 16

EXECUTIVE BIOGRAPHY

WORK HISTORY

1973 - present   Vice President - Controller
                   ABC Company
                   Chicago, Illinois

1970 - 1973   Division Controller
                   Alpha Division
                   XYZ Corporation
                   Minneapolis, Minnesota

1968 - 1970   Controller
                   Alpha Company
                   Minneapolis, Minnesota

1965 - 1968   Cost Control Manager
                   Theta Manufacturing, Inc.
                   Minneapolis, Minnesota

1962 - 1965   Certified Public Accountant
                   Roberts and Smith, CPA's
                   Minneapolis, Minnesota

EDUCATION   B.A. (Accounting) 1960
                   University of Minnesota

PROFESSIONAL
QUALIFICATIONS   C.P.A., 1962

PROFESSIONAL   American Management Association
ASSOCIATIONS   American Institute of CPAs
                   National Association of Accountants

viewing a person who has submitted a resume that includes a photograph, and the reason is simple. No one wants to be accused of interviewing on the basis of personal preference or hiring in violation of the Equal Rights Amendment any more than they want to be caught rejecting or firing an employee for reasons of race, creed, color, or nationality.

FAMILY. Don't include information about your family. Who cares if your wife's name is Veronica and your son Timmie is eleven? Since this type of information has no bearing on your ability to perform, it has no place in your resume.

NICKNAME. Don't mention your nickname. You can use it *after* you get the job, Corky.

LENGTH.   Don't let your resume exceed two pages. One page is preferable.

PAPER.   Use white or off-white letter-size sheets of good-quality stock.

TITLES.   Don't categorize yourself—unless, of course, you are using the resume for a particular position; in that case, you should definitely categorize. But if you are concentrating on accomplishments, as you should be, then de-emphasize titles and classifications.

HOBBIES.   Be careful about listing hobbies. Anytime you list a hobby you run the risk of offending someone or causing concern to the recipient of your resume. So why volunteer information that might be controversial? It's an unnecessary risk that might potentially have negative consequences. For example, skydiving might be considered a perfectly acceptable form of spare-time activity by some employers, but to others, it might seem much too risky.

PHYSICAL DESCRIPTION. If your health is excellent, say so. But listing your height and weight serves no purpose. If you are 6 feet 3 inches tall and weigh 235 pounds you might just intimidate yourself out of an interview with a ninety-seven-pound weakling, who might happen to be in charge of one of your strongest target companies.

ASSOCIATIONS. It's okay to list service clubs, professional or trade groups, fraternities, and sororities, but go easy on such things as charity organizations or religious groups that might prove to be controversial. And, by all means, don't mention political affiliations. If you put employers in a position where they might later be accused of hiring or not hiring you on the basis of politics (or race or religion or just about anything else except your qualifications), you are asking for an immediate rejection. If you have a private pilot's license, don't list it unless you are sure you are on safe ground. The recipient may consider it a high-risk activity. And forget athletics unless you were an All-American. It is best to include only those credentials and affiliations that could have a direct and positive effect on your job qualifications.

EDUCATION. If you have a weak academic background, play it down. If you have a strong one, emphasize it. Don't overstate or understate but do present yourself in the most favorable light. Mention your high-school education only if you attended a top-notch private school. Be careful about listing trade or vocational schools, and if you are uncertain about its effect on your resume, don't list it at all. Don't list private courses in sales, public speaking, real estate, insurance, motivation, and so on unless they are well-known and highly regarded. Employers tend to pooh-pooh the filler stuff—and with good reason.

In most cases you should start the list with business schools and junior colleges, then follow with universities and colleges. If you did not receive a degree, don't mention the dates you attended. Simply state your major and minor subjects, along with the name and location of the school. Don't mention your grade-point averages unless you were in the upper ten percent of your class. If you are very young, with little or no job experience, you probably should take full advantage of your educational background, since there may be little else to write about.

When you list your degree (or degrees), save the advanced education until last. Don't list "equivalent" work. If you have it, fine; but don't insult the intelligence of a prospective employer by trying to fool him. Persons with degrees may wish to state their major and minor areas of concentration, depending upon the company and position under consideration. But by no means should you enclose a copy of your thesis or mention your I.Q.

AGE.   This is one of the most sensitive items on a resume. You are almost certain to be either too old or too young in the eyes of the person who is reading your resume. Unless you are sure that your age is right for the job, leave it off. An age problem can best be handled in person. The omission may create some suspicion, but if your resume is well-done, it probably won't cost you an interview. If you think your age is a problem, be especially careful not to date yourself when you mention your education or employment history. And don't list your place of birth or the fact that you are a United States citizen. These things are irrelevant and have no place in your resume.

If you are concerned that by omitting your age you will forfeit an interview, remember that you should not be using your resume to obtain interviews in the first place. If you are on your toes you will get interviews in spite of your resume, not because of it. (If it doesn't get in your way it has served its purpose —remember?)

MARITAL STATUS. If you are single, divorced, separated, or a widow or widower, leave it off. If you are married and have three children, say so, but don't mention your children's ages, and don't say that you have been married for "ten blissful years" (although that can be considered a real achievement).

ADDRESS AND PHONE NUMBER. Include your area code with your phone number and your zip code with your address. If you feel that your address shows you in an unfavorable light, use a post-office box. Stating that you own your home or that you are renting or that you have lived in the same house for sixteen years is unnecessary and will only clutter up your resume. Omit any reference to an apartment number or mobile home space if you can receive your mail without it.

MILITARY. Don't mention your draft or reserve status. Nowadays, it is no longer a necessary qualifier. Leave your service record off in most cases. Even if you have had a full military career, be careful about saying so in your resume. Most companies have not yet learned how to translate military positions into their civilian counterparts, and you may not get the opportunity to do it for them. Generally speaking, the less you say about your military history the better, since employers tend to categorize the military along with other "non-profit" organizations such as Civil Service and you might find yourself on the outside looking in.

Here's a special word for you if you have a twenty- or thirty-year military career behind you and you're faced with the problem of selling yourself in the civilian marketplace. Whether you're aiming for employment in the area of Food Service or Program Management, the civilian vocabulary contains a match for each and every military counterpart position. And if you don't know the language you'd better learn it . . . fast! Be sure to make the translation yourself and don't rely on a civilian employer to do it accurately (if at all).

A friend of mine, a highly qualified ex-Colonel, had enjoyed an exceptional Air Force career with heavy emphasis on program control, configuration management, sensor engineering, quality assurance, reliability and maintainability, production control, and appropriations management. Any number of fine companies should have jumped at the chance to hire this man, but after four dog and pony shows the interviewers were still asking "But what can you really do?" (Why should I hire you?)

And remember, you aren't selling experience. In fact, you don't really have experience to sell. It's true that you have *had* experiences and that those experiences were instrumental in the development of your talents, but now you must market your abilities, *not* your experience.

Most military jobs have counterpart positions in the civilian world, and these parallels are usually recognizable. In some cases, however, the retiring military person may have to deal in the not-so-obvious. For example, a successful platoon leader is certainly qualified to deal with people, to motivate them, to manage them, to inspire them, and, most important, to lead them. He's an expert at getting maximum performance from his people under extremely adverse conditions. He will have developed valuable expertise in the area of human behavior. In short, he knows excellence as the Order of the Day, and his loyalty and integrity are above question. I could go on and on, but I'm sure you are getting the message. Incorporate your military accomplishments and talents into your approach to the civilian job market, and you might be surprised how much you have going for yourself. Ironically enough, the major problem with ex-military people when entering the civilian job market isn't a shortage of transferable talents but rather a reluctance on the part of military people to fully shed their military habits. For example, a person who stubbornly hangs on to such typical military jargon as 0900 hours or "Sir" is clearly having a little trouble taking off his uniform. Perhaps owing to fear and uncertainties about the job market, the military retiree may have an unusually tough time cutting the umbilical cord. Another common mistake made by the ex-military is to consult with other active and retired military and expect productive advice. I don't mean to imply that military experience is not a valid and important background; I'm simply saying that it should be played down in most resumes (and in most interviews).

SALARY.   You shouldn't ordinarily include your salary history or present salary requirements in your resume. If you do, you might deal yourself out of some important dollars. In general, try to avoid discussing salary either verbally or in writing—at least until you have received a tentative job offer.

So how do you handle the salary question when you mail your resume in response to an advertisement? First of all, you should send your resume only in very rare instances. Send a letter instead, and omit any mention of salary. And be careful not to spend much time answering ads (not more than ten minutes each), for it seldom pays off and can even prove harmful. (Companies sometimes advertise an opening when in fact the opening doesn't even exist. This is sometimes done merely as a favor to a friend in a competing firm who wants to test an employee's loyalty. If you answer such an ad, you might learn that your resume has found its way back to your boss's desk. Or worse yet, you may not find out.)

EMPLOYMENT HISTORY.   Forget this phrase, and call it a "brief summary of accomplishments." In some cases, depending on the circumstances, you should leave out the dates of employment altogether. A record of short-term positions can be a negative. So modify it—don't always list the "from" and "to" dates. Think in terms of qualifications, experience, accomplishments, and problem-action-results (P.A.R.). If you have had no job titles that do justice to your previous authority and responsibility, don't mention titles at all. If you have worked for companies that have a questionable reputation, don't mention company names. And if your present employer doesn't know you are job hunting, don't mention your present company by name.

Be careful about listing cumulative experience in a given position or responsibility. If you state that you have had "seventeen years' combined experience" as a purchasing agent and that you are still a purchasing agent, you are in trouble. Try something like this: "Each of my seventeen years as a professional in purchasing shows increased authority, responsibility, and profit." Or: "The most recent five years of my seventeen-year career in purchasing includes complete responsibility for annual budgets of $14,000,000 and over." Or: "In seventeen years of purchasing experience, I advanced from clerk to a $14,000,000 budget responsibility, reporting directly to the president. And each year I bettered my employer's goals."

Most prospective employers are not too interested in the things you have done in the *past* unless those achievements are somehow directly applicable to their particular situation. What does interest them is what you can do for their company in the *future. Present your accomplishments and emphasize bottom-line results*—the direct or indirect effect you have had on profits. Your resume should include words such as savings, profit, financial, budget, net, gross, dollar amount, objective, fiscal, monetary, revenue, money, cost reduction, achieve, earnings, bottom line, percentage, discount, increase, goal, decrease, improve, update, incorporate, initiate, execute. Even a shipping clerk with no one to supervise has an indirect effect on profits. If he reduces shipping time from four days to two days without increasing overhead, he can claim a money accomplishment. It shows up in better customer relations, in improved relations between his company's sales and shipping departments, and in total revenue increases. You might not be able to accurately measure this feat in terms of precise profit, but you can say something like: "Eliminated routing orders through secretary by installing telephone in warehouse. Within three days reduced shipping time from four to two days. Within six months sales increased three percent to $14,000,000 without affecting overhead." Even well-done resumes are dangerous, and without accomplishments to back them up, they can be lethal.

REASONS FOR LEAVING PAST OR PRESENT JOB. Don't mention them until the interview. (More on this subject later.)

REFERENCES. Phrase it this way: "Outstanding references and verification of accomplishments." Leave the details until later. Then be sure you have *thoroughly* cleared the matter with your references and that they are eager to help. Not just willing, but eager.

If you possibly can, get one good, strong letter from each of your references. Such a letter should be a hard-hitting recommendation containing substantial details and offering to discuss you at length with potential employers. Don't hesitate to help by writing the letter yourself. Here's an important point: *You will probably never show the letters to anyone.* The idea is to get commitments from which your references cannot later depart. This tactic is especially important with present and past employers. Be sure to get in touch with each reference, preferably in person, and know exactly how he or she will respond to an inquiry. Make your approach when your relationship with your reference is at a high point. Time has a way of diluting the quality and potency of references, especially if they receive many inquiries, so don't weaken your references by overusing them.

After you receive your letters of recommendation, be sure to acknowledge them with a reciprocal letter. For example:

Dear Dick:
Your recommendation is just what I needed, and quite frankly I'm flattered that you think so highly of my abilities. I'll be careful not to impose upon your time by using it any more than is essential.

Many thanks,

Henry

Then follow up after two weeks with a note like this one:

Dear Dick:
I've had some interesting interviews but haven't actually accepted anything yet.
Your name has proved to be a real plus factor, and your range of fans is broader than you might think.
Thanks again, Dick, for your interest in my career.

Henry

P.S. There's a rumor that the Reynolds firm plans to expand their Far East market. Have you heard anything about it?

Then later:

Dear Dick:
   Thanks for your input on Reynolds. I had a chat with Ed Jensen, their V.P. of International Marketing, and he confirmed your thoughts. Their expansion is at least a year away, and I'm not interested in waiting, but I sure appreciate the lead.
   I'm also interested in Wilmington Fabrications (Denver), Scott Arlington and Company (Portland), and E.E. Tyson here in town. Can you offer some comments on these firms? Since you were formerly with Tyson and since they are local, it might be a natural. Once again, many thanks.

Personal regards,
Henry

By now you begin to get the picture. Obtain as many outstanding references as you can—top people in companies that can at least indirectly offer you the opportunities you want. Then cultivate them, nurture them, and make them a prominent part of your job search. Use a large number of references, for these are your best sources of job opportunities—within their own companies as well as within others. Once you have obtained a favorable recommendation from your references, keep in close touch with them. In this way, your references become your target. They have already passed judgment on your desirability, and there is every reason to assume you might become a potential job candidate for them—or for someone else in their firm. After all, how many companies can you find in which the top person has already interviewed and personally endorsed you? And you will probably end up with

ILLUSTRATION 17

a more attractive compensation package—and even preferred treatment—in the future. Then, after you start your new job, maintain an on-going relationship with all your references, for therein may lie your future positions. Make sense? Think about it—a lot!

Don't separate "personal" references from "professional" references. If your reference isn't convinced that he knows you well enough to endorse you personally *and* professionally, you haven't handled him properly. It may take a couple of personal calls to get him into a position where you can really count on him, but the result will be worth the extra effort. Cultivating references is perhaps the most vital groundwork you will do.

JOB OBJECTIVE.   Leave it off your resume, or you will really be playing with fire. If you must submit a resume, define your objectives in a cover letter. Most objectives as set forth on resumes can be read with eyes closed:

> *"Seek growth-oriented position with company that can fully utilize my background and experience."*

> *"Want challenge and opportunity with creative and young-thinking company that will only settle for the best."*

Sound familiar? You bet they do because everyone is looking for the same thing. Who doesn't want challenge and opportunity? Put your objectives in your cover letter so you won't mar the composition of your resume. And whatever you do, go easy on your personal and professional objectives. Employers are interested primarily in what you can do for *them*, not what they can do for *you*.

As an alternative to meaningless job objectives, consider putting this kind of statement in your cover letter:

"From the description, your sales-manager position coincides perfectly with my qualifications and career objectives."

OR

"Judging from your ad, your needs and mine seem to have a lot in common. I'm as interested in changing the course of a sagging sales force as you are. That's my specialty."

OR

"I know what you mean. As a group, accountants aren't generally considered to be aggressive and innovative. But I broke out of that group right after I received my C.P.A. eight years ago. And now I am aiming for something with real potential."

Don't just write. Talk! And talk to be heard. If you don't make yourself stand out, who will? Throw out most of the old rules and be yourself. Don't use gimmicks, just speak freely and definitively on paper. And do it in your cover letter, *not in your resume.*

V.
INTERVIEWS:
A Time to Listen

_____
_____
_____
_____
_____
_____
_____
_____
_____
_____
_____
_____
_____
_____
_____
_____

GETTING INTERVIEWS

First off, "interview" isn't exactly the right word. Webster's dictionary defines an interview as "a formal consultation used to evaluate the aptitude, training, or progress of a student or prospective employee." When we seek an interview, we certainly don't want a "formal consultation," nor do we want to have our "aptitude, training, or progress" evaluated. Nor are we necessarily "students." The only part that seems to fit is "prospective employee."

Until someone comes up with a more appropriate term, let's assign our own definition to Webster's word: "an equal-level, face-to-face discussion between a job-seeker and a person with full authority to fill the position under discussion."

If you accept this definition, then you must agree that obtaining an interview is nothing more than gaining an audience for a discussion, or making an appointment. If you have ever made an appointment, you know that it is not a difficult task. Job-seekers, once they learn this simple truth, can easily fall victim to a contagious disease: too many interviews. The problem then is not how to get interviews but how to be selective and make each one count.

Referral System

For most people, the "third party," or "referral," system is probably the most effective means of obtaining interviews. Start by making a list of as many friends or acquaintances as you can think of who might be able to help. You should, by reaching a bit, be able to come up with fifty or a hundred names. Next, eliminate those people whom you don't want to contact because it might be embarrassing. The remaining names will provide you with an excellent referral source to get interviews. I don't know that I can tell you all the reasons for it, but most people will go out of their way to help even a total stranger get a job interview when given the chance.

Talk with each person on your list. By phone if need be, but in person if possible. Tell them about your plans to seek a new position, and enlist their help. If possible, encourage them to set interview appointments for you, rather than merely supply you with names. From your list of fifty or so friends, you should be able to get a number of interviews; however, most of these interviews will not necessarily be in keeping with your ambitions. But don't let this deter you. Remember that these "preliminary" interviews are primarily useful as a vehicle for obtaining *meaningful* interviews by referral. And don't overlook the possibility that the employers with whom you conduct your "preliminary" interviews might also be in the market to hire someone.

For the most part, your "preliminary" interviews will not succeed in actually producing a job offer for you, but that's to be expected. Once the interviewer has told you that he doesn't have an opening, or that you are overqualified, or underqualified, or whatever, give him a chance to be a hero. Ask for referrals (leads). Try something like this:

"Look, Mr. Thompson, you know more about me now than just about anyone else in town. Whom would you suggest I see?"

This approach takes him off the hook. After turning you down, the interviewer would ordinarily expect you to thank him and then depart with your tail between your legs. Instead, you must afford him an opportunity to compensate for the unpleasant task of turning you down for the job. You might even consider going a bit further, like this:

"Since you are a friend of Mr. Jones (to whom you are being referred), *I'm sure a phone call from you would mean a lot more than one from me. Would you mind giving him a try?"*

You'll probably discover that he is only too happy to accommodate you. You might also find out that he will volunteer a high recommendation to his referral, even though he may not actually be well-acquainted with your qualifications.

Work each referral in much the same fashion. Never accept a turn-down in a job interview without trying your best to obtain additional referrals and recommendations. But remember, you won't get referrals *unless you ask* for them. And after an interview with a referral, write or call the person who gave you the referral, and tell him about the results. *Then ask for more referrals.*

Decent Exposure

Exposure is all-important in getting interviews. If you are active, well-read, and aware, that's great! But you must also be alert. Almost everything you do, almost everyone you talk with, almost everything you hear or see or read has the potential to lead to an interview.

As an example, take the case of Keith Riehmer (the name is fictitious but the story isn't). Keith had worked for several years in Chicago as a production supervisor for a medium-sized manufacturer of cardboard boxes and other woodbase containers. His salary was $16,000, and at age thirty-six he was just about breaking even. He and his wife decided they wanted to move to the West Coast. A few months later, they settled in San Francisco with their two children. Upon his arrival, Keith's assets amounted to a one-year-old car, a B.A. in business from a fairly good school, a Kiwanis button, and forty-two hundred dollars (from the sale of his home). After renting a small house and enrolling the children in school, he prepared a resume and set out to fulfill his dream. He could describe exactly what he wanted: "A growth-oriented position

ILLUSTRATION 18

with a company that can fully utilize my background and experience." He also wanted "challenge" and "opportunity," because he knew he was "results-oriented." (Same old story.)

Five months later he was still results-oriented and still looking for a job. He had hit nearly every employment agency and recruiting firm in town. He had answered ads, sent letters and resumes to any and all potential employers, placed two ads of his own in the local paper, and even started attending church to increase his contacts. Meanwhile, his wife had resumed her teaching career by accepting an assistant professorship at a local university and, while she tried to understand Keith's dilemma, she suspected that somehow he wasn't doing everything he could be doing to find a new position. Further complications set in when Keith began comparing his own "luck" to that of his industrious wife. And sensing her disappointment in his failure to find work, his self-image really took a nosedive. Finally, in desperation he began the self-defeating exercise of lowering his sights and interviewing for jobs that were below his potential. He still got no results—this time because he was overqualified. He worked for a while as a part-time salesman, then made up a new resume calling himself a "consultant"—another word for unemployed.

His days gradually took on a standard routine: He got up, dressed, left the house, and went off in search of a place to take refuge until five o'clock at which time he could return home and lie to his family about his day's activities, One such spot, which eventually became a regular hiding place for Keith, was the local office of a top securities broker, which he stumbled into partly out of curiosity but chiefly because no one was charging admission. During trading hours, the offices of most securities brokers offer some pretty interesting entertainment. Seats are lined up as in a theater, and the stage consists of lighted boards that tell the spectators when to laugh and when to cry. The show attracts a wide variety of spectators, some of whom, like Keith, are not even investors.

At last, Keith was doing what he should have done months earlier. He took a seat between two observers in the spectator section of the brokerage office. The observer to his left, Observer A, turned out to be a mere spectator (like himself). But the observer to his right, Observer B, looked like he was onto something, and, after spotting in his lap the annual report for a company Keith had never heard of, he decided to initiate a conversation. He inquired about the company, and B was happy to respond. As it turned out, the firm was primarily involved in commercial agriculture and had recently acquired a small company that manufactured, installed, and maintained high-quality irrigation systems. Keith learned that B usually dropped into the broker's "theater" each trading day about eleven o'clock. Over a period of several days, the two became quite friendly and had lunch together twice. B, who was thinking of investing in the subject company himself, had done a thorough investigation, and gladly shared his findings with Keith. This prompted Keith to do some research on his own. Within a few more days, he had completed his homework and determined how he could best serve the company.

All the necessary ingredients were there. The firm fit his desired profile, and, since it was based in San Francisco, it seemed to be a natural. Completely ignoring his resume, he fired off a letter to the president of the company stating that he had studied the company in depth, had developed a keen interest, and would call his secretary in two days to arrange an appointment. He followed through with the secretary and, after being pushed aside twice, finally got his appointment, gained additional information, defined his role with the company, handled three separate interviews, and went on board as Assistant to the Vice President in charge of production at a starting salary of $21,000.

Keith's experience contains some important lessons. Anyone could fault his performance up to the point where he dropped in at the broker's office, so let's pick it up from that point. Whether by accident or otherwise he started doing a few things right:

1. *Exposure*. He actually ventured into a strange environment that was known to house commercial information and opportunity. He took a seat *between two people* and didn't isolate himself. He started a conversation with one of the two and didn't give up when it proved fruitless. (Exposure comes *before* opportunity.)

2. *Opportunity*. He developed a sincere interest in the company, its activities, its people, and its product. He looked at the good and bad points through the eyes of an investor. He took more than a surface look, visualizing himself in the position of "Assistant to the Vice President of Production" even though that position didn't even exist. He knew the salaries and fringe benefits of the company and the

salary range within which he could reasonably expect to negotiate. He knew the company's operations and its plans for the future, and he had a good idea of its strategies for getting there. His information also included a rundown on the company's competition and some inside information that Observer B had managed to pry out of the company's banker, attorney, accountant, advertising agent, and transfer agent. B had even talked with customers of the company, which helped in pinpointing the firm's weak areas.

From that point on, Keith's chores were clear cut. He had to:

1. Make an appointment with the decision-maker (an interview).
2. Gather as much information from the interview as possible (exposure).
3. Point out the company's problems and his ability to solve them (create opportunity).
4. Define the position to the decision-maker.
5. Close (get the job).

One of the most important points illustrated by Keith's story is that although he didn't know it at the time, the job Keith had been looking for simply didn't exist. Lousy odds, right? Just think of it: a qualified man (in the market for a position) who had been doing everything wrong to get a job that wasn't even there! And sadly enough, the only thing un- usual about Keith's story is that it had a happy ending—or rather a happy beginning: his new job. Indeed, the woods are full of Keith Riehmers, people who are competing unneces-

Remember: Getting interviews is nothing more than making appointments.

sarily for the same jobs and canceling out one another's efforts.

Companies are really only groups of people: small groups, medium-sized groups, and large groups composed of individual personalities, and having unique problems, strengths, and weaknesses. And companies, like the people that comprise them, are always changing. A company that isn't growing is going backward, and you shouldn't waste your time with it —except in those rare cases that offer a turn-around opportunity at the highest level of management. For the most part, you should direct your attention toward companies that are on the move and that are expanding within prominent growth industries. Don't forget that almost every skill is transferable, not just from company to company, but from industry to industry and from business to business. So you needn't be saddled forever to a losing industry.

Again, getting interviews is really very simple, and you should *never stop interviewing*. It is not unusual to hear people say something to this effect: "This is the first time I've ever had to look for a job. Companies have always sought me out, or I've known about an available position and just sort of moved into it." That's rubbish, of course, because had these people not been interested (or looking), they would never have listened. And they certainly would not have pursued the position to the point of accepting it had their minds been closed to making a change. That's exposure. Any time you are offered a position, it's because you first gained exposure, even if by accident.

And now we're right back to the basics. *You must first gain EXPOSURE and then create OPPORTUNITY, for that's what getting a job is all about.* You must "interview" to gain exposure, and you must create opportunity to get job offers.

We all possess the necessary qualities, such as courage, persistence, ambition, and creativity. Getting interviews depends largely upon how much of each quality you are willing to let work for you. If you really want interviews, you will have to exercise these qualities, since the number of interviews you get will always be directly proportionate to your efforts. Ironically, using these talents makes them grow stronger and more effective, which, in turn, affords you even bigger cannons in your career arsenal.

The Numbers Game

Obtaining job offers is largely a matter of averages. Let's say, for the sake of discussion, that you have selected thirty-six companies with which you would like to interview. You won't bat 1,000 percent of course, but you should be able to obtain interviews with at least seventy-five percent of your total, or twenty-seven companies. Out of the twenty-seven companies with which you interview, you will probably arrange a second interview

———————————

———————————

———————————

———————————

———————————

———————————

———————————

———————————

———————————

———————————

———————————

———————————

———————————

———————————

———————————

———————————

———————————

———————————

with only about one-third, or nine companies. Out of the nine companies that give you a second interview, you will probably achieve a third or fourth interview with about two-thirds, or six companies. Out of the final six companies, you should obtain no fewer than two firm job offers—a little better than one out of twenty original companies. Bear in mind that before you interview with any of these companies, you should have already determined that they fit your company profile and that they have something worthwhile to offer you.

Thanks for the Interview, Mr. Bell

If you are seeking interviews with a fairly large number of companies, the quickest way to get them is by placing direct telephone calls to the decision-makers themselves—*cold calls*. In order to get interviews from these cold calls, just about anything is permissible as long as you do not lie or misrepresent yourself. Some difficulty usually arises when it comes to getting around the decision-maker's secretary, who is often much more protective of the boss's time than the boss is. If you do have trouble getting through, here are some tactics you might consider:

SECRETARY: Good morning. Mr. Thompson's office.

CALLER: This is Henry Fowler. Is Mel in, please?

SECRETARY: Mr. Thompson is in conference. May I help you?

CALLER: No, I'll have to speak directly to Mel. What time do you expect that he'll be free?

SECRETARY: Well, I really don't know, Mr. Fowler, but tell me what the call is about, and I'll get word to him as soon as I can.

CALLER: Just tell him that Hank Fowler called and that I'll try to reach him again late this afternoon.

SECRETARY: Very well, Mr. Fowler, but I will need to advise Mr. Thompson as to the nature of the call.

CALLER: Quite frankly, this is a personal call and I would appreciate it if you would simply give him my message.

Then call back when you think the decision-maker might be available, and try again to arrange an appointment.

There are any number of possible variations on this conversation, of course, but the important points are these:

● Be friendly and courteous but nonetheless firm and authoritative with the secretary. Don't let this person decide whether or not you should talk with the boss. It's not so much what you say but rather the way you say it.

● Let the secretary know in a polite way that your call is *personal* and that it is really not anyone else's business.

● When the decision-maker is not available, leave your name so that when you call back it won't be as a total stranger.

● Don't leave your telephone number. If *you* place the call you have the added advantage of being prepared to talk. If the intercepting secretary insists on having your telephone number, simply say, "I'm sorry, I won't be able to be reached. I'll have to call *him*."

● Generally, you should refer to the decision-maker by his first name when talking with his secretary. Be careful, however, about continuing on a first-name basis once you have actually reached the decision-maker (at least until it is warranted by the situation).

● If the decision-maker happens to be out of town for a week, no harm done. Simply drop him a brief, well-written, typed letter stating that you have been unsuccessful in your attempts to reach him but will try again when he returns. Then follow through on schedule. Do not enclose your resume with the letter.

● Making cold telephone calls to decision-makers can be a frightening experience for some people. Remember, however, that you are still dealing with percentages. And if your ego is so sensitive that you can't face an occasional rejection, then you may not really belong where you think you'd like to be. Talking to the secretary usually isn't so bad, and most people can handle it without much difficulty. But once the decision-maker is on the line it's quite another matter. Most people freeze up simply because they think of themselves as the seller, and the decision-maker as the buyer. And in a buyer/seller situation the buyer has the advantage, right? Wrong! As a matter of fact, the advantage belongs to the person who *controls* the conversation, regardless of whether he is the buyer or the seller.

● *Relax*, think of the human being on the other end of the line. Not the position, not the authority, not the responsibility, not the money. Just the person. Who knows? He may be more fearful than you are. The trick is to talk *with* him and not *at* him. And keep your call brief, friendly, firm, and to the point. Remember, the only reason you are calling is to set up an appointment, an equal-level discussion between you and the decision-maker. Above all, don't allow him to interview you over the telephone. (A telephone interview is about the quickest way in the world to get a turn-down.)

Here is a sample conversation (once you have succeeded in getting past the secretary):

CALLER: Mr. Thompson?

DECISION-MAKER: Yes.

CALLER: Mr. Thompson, my name is Hank Fowler. I'm gathering some information on the (banking) industry, and since I understand that you're about the best and the busiest around, I'd appreciate a little help.

DECISION-MAKER: Well, Mr. Fowler, what can I do for you?

CALLER: I have a couple of ideas that I'd like to run by you, and perhaps we can pick each other's brains a bit. I'm a banker too, so I know how impossible schedules can get, but if you have a few minutes within the next day or two, give me a time and I'll drop by.

DECISION-MAKER: What specifically do you have in mind, Mr. Fowler?

_____
_____
_____
_____
_____
_____
_____
_____
_____
_____
_____
_____
_____
_____
_____
_____
_____
_____
_____

CALLER: Let me say simply that it's a highly personal matter and one that will best be discussed in person. Since I'm not selling anything, I suppose I seem a bit persistent, but you're the only one who can really answer my questions. Are the mornings or the afternoons usually better for you?

DECISION-MAKER: The afternoons are generally better, but I'll be tied up in the afternoons until Thursday.

CALLER: All right, Mr. Thompson, suppose I drop over Thursday afternoon about three-thirty?

DECISION-MAKER: All right, Mr. Fowler, I'll put you on my calendar for that time.

If you look closely, you will notice a bit of double-talk, but it is within bounds, since the only reason you are making the call is to set up an appointment. Here are some other points to note about this hypothetical conversation:

- You have addressed the decision-maker as "Mister," but only twice during the entire conversation. Even if he calls you by your first name, it is usually a good idea not to use his first name until after you have met him in person.
- You have not lied or misrepresented yourself.
- You haven't divulged the nature of the appointment.

- You have established some credibility by letting him know that you are knowledgeable in his field.
- You have let him know that you can't be shuttled off to a junior officer.
- You have displayed tenacity and determination, and have not forfeited your objective (you score a couple of points just for determination).
- You have offered an alternative in setting up a time but no alternative in setting up an appointment.
- Most important you have set up the appointment.

Don't worry about what might happen if he challenges you at the first appointment on your method of getting in to see him. After all, you got the job done—which is worth something to him as well as to you. Later, when it becomes apparent that you are really interviewing for a position, he may again remind you of the fact that you allowed him to assume whatever he chose in your initial telephone call. This is just his attempt to even the scales and to save his own ego. He knows that you didn't lie, that in fact you did an effective selling job on him. Respond with a statement to this effect: "You're the only man in this organization that has sole authority to discuss a position with me, and, quite frankly, that was about the only honest way I knew of getting to you."

Even if a first interview doesn't warrant a second, be sure to use it as an opportunity to obtain leads (additional interviews), and don't be bashful. When an interview goes sour, ask for counsel and guidance; then turn the conversation toward leads.

INTERVIEWING

Although most employers consider themselves to be expert at interviewing, very few really know much about it. They usually begin an interview like this: "Well, Henry, tell me a little bit about yourself." If you don't know any better, you will answer him and then you've blown it. A first interview should be an exploratory conversation to validate the information you have gathered and to determine whether you are interested in a second interview. Make sure that it remains an *equal-level* discussion. Be yourself. The interviewer will expect you to be on your toes, so don't disappoint him. But don't jump up and light his cigar or pull his chair out for him. The interviewer will also expect you to be a bit nervous—and you won't disappoint him!

Be prepared before the first interview to ask at least six pertinent questions about the company and its operations. (Remember, you're gathering information; you're not selling anything yet—at least not openly.) Your questions should relate directly to the past, present, and future internal workings of the firm. Direct the questions toward sensitive areas: profits, competition, collections, growth, government regulations, patents, labor relations, increasing and decreasing markets, increased expenses, technical limitations. Don't be afraid to put the interviewer on the spot. If you handle the discussion in an honest and professional manner, he will respect you for it. You *must* be able to pinpoint his problems; otherwise, how can you help resolve them?

As you gain information during the interview, mentally match that information with what you learned on your own prior to the interview. You will quickly reach some preliminary conclusions about whether or not to seek a second interview.

Here's Looking at You!

In all of your interviews, be sure to maintain proper eye contact. Don't stare, but in a relaxed fashion look into the other person's eyes. You should be able to comfortably maintain eye contact for at least eight seconds, with lookaway intervals of not more than two seconds. When you do shift your eyes away from the interviewer, make sure you shift your body at the same time. Otherwise you might seem to have "shifty" eyes.

Here's a pointer for you if you have a problem in maintaining proper eye contact. If you

ILLUSTRATION 19

are over five or six feet from the interviewer, he won't notice it if you look at the bridge of his nose rather than directly into his eyes. Most people when eye-balling one another look at a left eye or right eye. Very rarely both eyes at the same time, unless the two parties are actually nose to nose. Shift your target from the interviewer's right (or left) eye, and concentrate on the area between his eyes. It might be a great deal more comfortable for you while still helping you to communicate trust and credibility.

Talking Torso

Don't be a maestro with flapping arms. Gestures are most effective if they are infrequent and natural. Frequent gesturing puts the interviewer's attention on your gyrations, not on you.

Regardless of what you think you know about body language, sit with the base of your spine against the back of your chair. This position offers you the best and most practical opportunity to present yourself naturally and effectively. So long as you keep your lower back in the correct position, you can throw most of the remaining rules of proper body language out the window. If you are a male, you probably won't be able to cross your legs from that position and that's all right. You can still move your arms freely and lean forward with ease. And of course, don't smoke, chew gum, or fidget.

Your own attention should be focused on the interviewer. Make a mental note of his suit, his shirt, his tie, his complexion, his eyes, his hair, and his body language. Force yourself to look closely enough to get the details. If he folds his arms and crosses his legs, you may be in trouble (defensive and negative). Change the subject, and help him relax, but make a mental note of the circumstance that made him uncomfortable so that you can use it as ammunition a little later on. Remember that most people who interview you are not professional interviewers and have little idea how to handle the situation, so it's usually an awkward experience for both of you.

Don't be overly humble or assume a demeaning role. And don't be overly aggressive or cute. If your interest, sincerity, or strength is in doubt, you won't have a chance.

On rare occasions you may encounter an interviewer who puts you at a physical—and psychological—disadvantage by facing you into a bright light or by having you sit in a chair with a lower elevation than his own. Or you may find that the only available chair is across the room and at an awkward angle. Or the interviewer may be constantly interrupted by telephone calls or visitors. When these things happen, take matters into your own hands. Move the chair to a comfortable position. If the sun is in your eyes, reposition your chair or suggest that the drapes be pulled. If constant interruptions preclude an effective interview, simply stand up and say, "Mr. Thompson, I've obviously caught you at a bad time. Why don't you suggest a time tomorrow afternoon when you won't be quite so pressed?" He will either set up a new appointment or see to it that the interruptions stop. In either case, you have gained. To continue under such conditions is out of the question, and if he is not really serious about the interview, you might as well know it at the outset.

_____
_____
_____
_____
_____
_____
_____
_____
_____
_____
_____
_____
_____
_____
_____
_____
_____
_____

Always try to keep the ball in your opponent's court. These hypothetical conversations illustrate how it's done:

INTERVIEWER: Henry, you've been with three separate firms during the past five years.

INTERVIEWEE: And every one a winner, Mel. In a short time I've gained the background it could have taken thirty years to acquire. When you check my references, you'll find that I would still be there had I not outgrown the job. Now, if you don't mind, I'd like to have your views on individual growth within *your* company.

OR

INTERVIEWER: Quite frankly, Henry, we are looking for someone a bit younger. Fifty-two isn't over the hill, but the average age on our team is thirty-seven.

INTERVIEWEE: You're right, Mel. It isn't over the hill. If it were possible to gain thirty years of job experience by the age of thirty-seven, it might be dangerous without the other maturities and seasoning that a man picks up along the way. A working blend of youth and experience is a pretty profitable combination:

And I have plenty of time left for a full career, so I don't want to stop growing. Now, how do *you* feel about growth opportunities for people who produce?

Of course, you can't turn every negative into a positive. Basically, your ploy has to make sense. But if you are aware of your weak areas and respond in a way that shows you in the best possible light, you are less apt to be pushed into a corner. If you have an obvious negative feature, such as age, and the interviewer fails to call it to your attention, he probably isn't leveling with you. So do some probing, and bring the subject up yourself. Ask him about the ages of your potential colleagues and how long they have worked for the firm. The idea is to determine their approximate ages at the time they were hired. Do your probing carefully so that you don't create a negative unnecessarily. Then, as soon as you are reasonably sure that your [age] will not cause a problem later, get on with your interview. Ask one of your prepared questions that will make the interviewer do the talking. And while he's talking, make mental notes that will help supply you with more questions. In this way, you will be able to maintain control of the interview.

There are few hard and fast rules in this book. However, here is one that simply must not be broken. During a job interview, *never talk about yourself for more than sixty seconds at a time*. Sound tough? It's not, really, with a little practice. Time yourself during a mock interview with your spouse or a friend. When it is necessary or advisable to talk about yourself, limit that part of your conversation to sixty seconds, and then regain control of the interview by asking a pertinent question.

An attorney friend of mine, Don Merkin, who is also the best authority on job interviewing I know, has an incredible system for regaining control of an interview. When the subject under discussion is uncomfortable, he advises his clients to get off the hot seat simply by saying, "That reminds me, Mr. Thompson," then ask one of your prepared questions. Don claims that to his knowledge no one has ever been called on this one—it always works.

When you are ready to start interviewing it's a good idea to experiment first with two or three companies that you don't really care about. Interview with them and test your interviewing talents. Don't be concerned about "blowing" these "practice" interviews; you can put the experience to good use in the really important interviews that follow. *Remember that job offers almost always go to the person who does the best job of getting the job and not necessarily to the person who is best qualified to do the job.*

The Rules of the Interview Game

Ordinarily you should go through at least three interviews with a company before making the decision to accept a job offer. Each interview should accomplish some specific objectives as you progress toward your final goal of starting to work for the company. Ideally the process will move about like this:

FIRST INTERVIEW
1. Make a good impression.

2. Get acquainted (warm up).
3. Gather information.
4. Define company problems.
5. Decide if you should seek a second interview.
6. Set up an appointment for a second interview (or obtain referrals).
7. Follow up with a thank-you letter.
8. Prepare and research for the second interview.

SECOND INTERVIEW
1. Warm up.
2. Recap first interview.
3. Discuss alternative solutions to company problems.
4. Discuss company competition.
5. Discuss company and industry future.
6. Trial close. (Ask for and try to get the job.)
7. Set up an appointment for a third interview (or obtain referrals).
8. Follow up with a thank-you letter or phone call.
9. Prepare for the third interview.

THIRD INTERVIEW
1. Warm up.
2. Trial close.
3. Recap first and second interviews.
4. Discuss your potential role in the company.
5. Pinpoint objections.
6. Overcome objections.
7. Close.
8. Negotiate compensation.
9. Final close and starting date.

FOURTH INTERVIEW
Any interview beyond the third should be merely a continuation of the negotiating and closing process.

Take It from the Top

Now let's dissect a few of these steps. *Make a good first impression (and second and third).* Your first shot is your best shot, of course, and it may be your only chance to win the favor of the interviewer, so do your best right from the start. But don't let your guard down after the first interview, even if your interviewer is shoddily dressed and seems to be unaware of his own appearance. After all, he's not interviewing for a job, and you won't help your cause if you mimic his bad habits in subsequent interviews.

WARM UP
This brief getting-acquainted period sets the tempo for an interview. Talk about common interests or friends, but keep it short. Although it is important to establish a good rapport, you should always keep your main objectives clearly in mind, and don't waste time. Not yours and not the interviewer's.

ADDITIONAL INFORMATION
Before the interview, you will have gathered as much information as possible regarding the company, its business, and its people. The interview offers you a chance to get the real inside dope and to confirm what you already know. Given the opportunity, most interviewers will talk at length about themselves and their company, even about matters that are sensitive or confidential. Company heads have been known to divulge very sensitive information while interviewing someone from a com-

peting firm, only to learn later that the interviewee took advantage of the situation. So ask pertinent questions, and listen to the answers. After all, you must decide quickly if you want another interview. And ultimately you might have to decide whether or not you want to work for the firm.

CLOSING AND TRIAL CLOSING
The term "closing" is more familiar to salespeople than to most others. It means closing the sale, or actually getting the order, or getting a yes from the buyer. In job interviewing its meaning is precisely the same. Closing is actually getting the job offer or getting a yes from the interviewer. It means closing the sale of your talents to the interviewer. Trial closing then, is nothing more than merely trying to close, trying to get the job offer.

If you are to sell your talents in the job market, you must be an effective closer and the key to closing is *desire*. You may very well possess the *need* to close, but that's not enough. You must have the *desire*. Good closers accept a turn-down as a challenge and recognize that "no" doesn't usually mean "no" but rather serves as an indication that the buyer isn't ready to buy. Those who have only the *need* to close obviously haven't received the message yet.

Can you imagine trying to close a job opportunity by saying "I've been four months without income, Mr. Thompson, and I simply must have a job"? Or maybe something like, "I realize I'm short on experience, Mr. Thompson, but after looking three months for a job I'm willing to give this position a try"? These approaches register the need in the wrong corner. *The need must be with the buyer, not the seller.* You must define the buyer's need, then satisfy that need. The desire and motivation to close must be the responsibility of the *interviewee*, not the *interviewer*.

The closing of a sale should be a natural, easy part of the entire sales process. It should neither be emotional nor uncomfortable. Build your case from the outset, and win on *minor* points along the way. NEVER put your interviewer in the position of having to make a major decision on the spot, for he is apt to react emotionally and negatively. Instead, work questions into the conversation that lead naturally into a closing opportunity and away from emotional traps. Here are some examples:

"How soon do you plan to fill the vacancy?"

"What other matters would you like to clear up before making a decision?"

"What's your timing?"

"Which other staff people do you want me to spend some time with during my first few days?"

"When may I meet the other people on the staff?"

"You said your annual meeting is in three days. If you have no objection I would like very much to attend as an observer. What time does it start?"

"It will take me about a week to wrap up some personal matters. How will that work out with your schedule?"

"It seems to me that the next step should be a thorough briefing by your controller. When will he be able to spend some time with me?"

"Are you ready to proceed now, Mel? Or have I failed to cover something with you?"

"Tell me, Mr. Thompson, exactly what stands between me and the position?"

As soon as you see some daylight, as soon as you smell smoke, as soon as you sense that your target is vulnerable—*CLOSE, CLOSE, CLOSE! Ask for the job!* Any number of job offers is lost simply because candidates don't ask for the job. One candidate went through five interviews with the same company president. At the start of the sixth interview, he blurted out in utter frustration: "Look, I've interviewed with you five times and this time I've come solely to ask for the job and won't be put off any longer." The response was immediate: "When can you start?"

ILLUSTRATION 20

Work on the assumption that your interviewer is going to hire you, and give him as much help as you can. To button up an offer, try using statements like these:

"Today is Friday, Mel, and I know you don't want to worry about filling this job over the weekend. So, unless I've failed to cover something, let's set Monday as my starting date."

"You'll be back from Chicago on the thirteenth, and I don't imagine you want this problem waiting for you when you return. So unless I've left some questions unanswered, let's plan my first day for the fifteenth."

"One of the firms I had considered is in a real spot, and, in fairness to them, I'd like to advise them this afternoon so they can start with someone else. Assuming that you have no further questions, why don't we set Monday as my first day?"

When you get a turn-down, don't give up. *Find out why.* Pinpoint the negatives, overcome them, and then try again to close.

Suppose an interviewer says to you: "Henry, you are an interesting person, and I'm sure you'll make a good man for the proper company, but in this case, you simply don't have enough experience in fiscal forecasting." He has done you a real favor. He could have turned you down without ever giving you the real reason. In effect, he has said that everything is fine (and that the job would be yours) if

only you had *enough* experience in fiscal forecasting. By isolating his objection he has made
it easy for you to handle. So handle it, and then
try to close. Remember, you haven't been told
"no." You have only been informed of an objection, not a rejection. And don't give up or ask
for leads until after you have tried every conceivable means to overcome his objection on
the spot. Here are a few suggestions:

*"When I went with Adams National three
years ago I knew much less about market
research than I know today about fiscal
forecasting and as you know, I was promoted
four times during that period and ended up
as head of the entire market research
department. We have a good start here, Mel,
and I think we both recognize that we'll make
a great team. Now, if you don't mind I'd like
to talk more about a starting date. What do
you think of the fifteenth?"*

*"Neither of us is a superman, Mel, but we are
both professionals and realistic. A man can
spend fifty years looking for the perfect wife,
but after that time he probably wouldn't have
the need even if he found her. Perfect I'm not,
but I* am *the man you need. What's your
deadline for having someone on board?"*

*"I could have thirty years of fiscal forecasting
behind me and it still wouldn't mean
anything unless I were really the man for the
job. If you were to take my three years of
experience and add twenty-seven to it I'd be
sixty-nine. A bit older than you'd probably
have in mind. Tell me, Mel, how did you
happen to join the firm?"*

"I'm glad you said "experience" and not "knowledge." Right now I have at least some experience and a lot of knowledge, and if you are actually deciding between experience and the ability to perform, it seems to me your choice is obvious. And here's a plus factor. My approaches are not old-fashioned. Personally, I don't subscribe to the philosophy that a company should "continue doing things in one particular way simply because things have always been done that way." If there's a better way, let's jump on it. Now, if you will, let's talk some more about the position. Where do you see it leading to in three years or five years?"

(And don't forget to limit your response to sixty seconds. The foregoing are less than thirty).

And Nothing But the Truth

Don't let the interviewer off the hook. Get to his *real* objections. Get them out in the open where you can deal with them. And after you handle each objection, don't wait for his nod of approval before you continue. Get right back in control of the interview with a question. Then set him up for another trial close.

An interviewer sometimes will put forth an objection that isn't really valid, such as "How do I know you won't leave after a year?" This and similar objections don't deserve a serious response. You might answer this way: "I can't promise you that I won't die either, Mel, but I will promise you that I'll try not to. When shall I start?"

You will find that most interviewers are afraid to commit their company. They are actually afraid to hire you. So they'll take the easy way out. They will raise objections. So expect objections, and deal with them. But don't be fooled by what the interviewer says. chances are that he isn't saying what he is really thinking. He may say you are over-qualified when he is really thinking that you would pose a threat to him. He may tell you that you are weak on experience when he re-ally thinks that you are too young. He may tell you he wants to talk with more candidates when in fact he is really concerned about justifying your salary to his boss. He may say that he doesn't have a spot for you when he is really concerned about your job-hopping record.

Try to understand the *real* reasoning behind his objections. Put yourself in his shoes. Probe gently into the underlying reasons behind his objections, deal with them, and help make it easy for him to hire you.

A person who is a strong closer will pick up where a weak closer leaves off. When you get a turn-down, look at it as a signal to get down to business. It takes brass to overcome a legiti-mate objection and then come right back with "When would you like for me to start?" But it takes even more brass for the interviewer to say, "I don't want you to start." Closing is a gutsy business and not for the fainthearted. Unless you are willing to develop your closing techniques, you might as well forget about everything else in this book. *Closing is the key*. And it can even be a lot of fun once you get the hang of it.

The biggest single reason for ineptness at closing is the fear of failure. Some people almost feed on unnecessary negatives such as these:

"What if he knows my boss?"

"I wonder if my divorce will be brought up?"

"What if I'm too young?"

"What if he asks me about my reason for changing jobs?"

"He's probably interviewed a lot of people who are better qualified than I am."

"My clothes aren't sharp enough."

"I wish I weren't so fat."

"Suppose they don't hire women for management jobs?"

"I'm not a good conversationalist."

"How will I respond if I'm asked about my salary history?"

"What if he doesn't agree with me?"

"He probably doesn't understand the military."

"What if he feels I don't have enough experience?"

"What if he thinks I'm too old?"

"I've never been good at interviewing."

"What if he finds out I was fired?"

"What if he thinks I'm stupid?"

"What if he doesn't need anyone?"

"Maybe I'm not really qualified."

"Maybe I'm overqualified."

"I'll probably tense up."

"He might not think I'm worth the money."

The fear of closing can ruin an otherwise promising career. Take the case of the woman real-estate broker who was quite effective in building a prospect's interest up to the point of showing a house. But once on the property, she immediately began to make excuses for her product. "The master bedroom is a little small but you could build an addition for not too much," she would say. Or, "The lawn is in pretty rough shape but I can line you up with a gardener." In truth, she was afraid of being turned down. She literally refused to put herself in a position where she had to sell rather than merely take an order. Little wonder that she was an outstanding failure. She had a *need* to close but lacked the *desire*. Her fear of rejection made closing nearly impossible.

Fortunately, the same weakness that prevents most people from becoming good closers is the very weakness that makes closing so easy. *Few people like to say no. And even fewer people have the stomach to slug it out with a good closer. And interviewers have the same weaknesses as interviewees;* they, too, have a fear of failure, of missing an opportunity by saying no to a promising and persuasive candidate. So take advantage of this factor to help you with your closing. Obtaining job offers involves two major steps: overcoming objections, then closing. So does every other type of selling. But remember that selling is not order-taking. Order-taking is merely saying yes to a job that is offered to you. Selling is getting the job offer you *want*—after overcoming objections —and then *closing*.

Hire Yourself a New Boss

When you go in for the close, make a positive statement of commitment that involves a definitive act on your part and that constitutes approval on the part of the interviewer (unless he stops you). Here are some examples:

"I'm going to hand in my resignation this afternoon, Mel, so why don't we plan on the fifteenth as my first day with you?"

OR

"I'll swing by the doctor's office first thing in the morning and get my physical out of the way so we won't be held up. Will the fifteenth work out all right for you?"

OR

"I'll use the rest of the day getting the kids transferred to the new school and report to you Monday morning at eight if that's okay."

OR

"I'm making a deposit on our new house this afternoon, and if you have a few minutes tomorrow morning, I'll drop by to finish up the salary thing."

You may feel that these statements sound pushy and don't really fit your personality. Perhaps they are a bit strong, but someone has to steer the ship, and if it's going to go where you want it to go, you will have to be in command. Gain control and keep control or you'll run aground.

Go over the above responses again very carefully. Note that they involve a certain amount of "talking in circles," but don't let it bother you. Your responses don't need to make sense; they just need to seem to make sense. If you speak with authority and conviction, if you are *believable*, the actual words will be secondary.

By now you should be familiar with the tactics that will get you the job you want. First, expect to get the job offer. Assume that you'll be hired. Then look for openings, and keep closing. Bring out the objections, overcome them, and then set up a trial close again by asking a question. Don't accept a turn-down as being final. *Keep closing.*

Stay alert for any kind of buying signal, no matter how weak. If your interviewer says "you would have to use the temporary office down the hall until we can make other arrangements," then assume that he is ready to close. "Fine, Mel," you might answer, "I've worked under much worse conditions. I'll see you on the fifteenth." Or he might say, "If this were six months from now we could certainly use you." Fine. Close the deal and then negotiate the starting date. If he says, "You would be working for a very demanding boss," that's great. Ask when you can meet him.

Don't try to close by presenting the interviewer with a yes-or-no situation. Don't make

> "Keep on going and the chances are you will stumble on something, perhaps even when you are least expecting it. I have never heard of anyone stumbling on something sitting down."
> Charles F. Kettering

him feel anxious about making a major decision. Move sideways into the closing and *close on minor points*. Afterward he may be unsure of how it happened, but he should have absolutely no doubt that he hired you.

Remember, *don't forget to ask for the job*. Too many times people walk away from a setup because they didn't finish the task at hand. If you have done your job in selling, then closing follows smoothly and comfortably. Even if you don't want the job, be sure to close. You can always say no later.

Shut Up and Get Out!

And what do you do after you close? Shut your mouth and get out. Don't be around when buyer's remorse sets in. Anything you do or say past the point of closing can be explosive. It has been said that the first person to speak *after* the close loses.

Never Stop Closing

In the job market you must be able to sell, and if you can't close, you can't sell. If you think you are not the "sales type," then you had better change your type immediately. No one can do the selling for you. In the final analysis, you are the person who wants the job, you are the one who must interview for the job, *you are the one who must close and negotiate compensation*, and you are the one who must say yes or no to a job offer.

Your career is *your* sole responsibility, and if you learn to be a good closer, you can call your own shots. You need never be concerned again about your ability to get a new and better job. You will have the least expensive insurance policy you can find.

VI.
SELECTION:
Take Your Choice

_____

_____

_____

_____

_____

_____

_____

_____

_____

_____

_____

_____

_____

_____

_____

_____

_____

TWO FOR THE MONEY

A single job offer provides no room for selection, so don't be quick to grab the first one that comes along. If you are fortified with two or three firm job offers, you have a much better opportunity to use one as insurance while negotiating the next. Use your leverage.

Go back to your short-term and long-term objectives, and force each offer to pass your scrutiny. If all other considerations are about equal, you will most likely make your choice on the basis of compensation, both short term and long term. This section covers final compensation negotiations, which will be vital to your selection.

Switcharoo

In negotiating salary the advantage goes emphatically to the interviewee—if he has done his work well. The ideal time to negotiate is *after* you have received the job offer but *before* the knot is tied. At this point, you suddenly find yourself converted from a seller to a buyer, and the rules are decidedly different.

Here's something worth repeating. Whenever possible, avoid talking salary—past or projected—until after you have been offered the job. Prior to that time, you may find it difficult to field such questions as "How much money are you looking for?" or "What was your last salary?" But you must avoid giving a direct answer, and if you are a good negotiator, you will be prepared to handle these questions. Here are some suggested responses:

"My principal concern is not with the starting salary but rather with the long-term

opportunity. I've been amply compensated in the past and, naturally, I expect to be in the future. However, I wouldn't want my salary history to stand in the way of this discussion." (Then ask a question.)

OR

"The compensation package is important, of course, and so are many other considerations. Personally, I like the feeling of growing with a company. I'd like to have an assignment that no one else wants and do it successfully. Or at least take on a difficult assignment and do it better than anyone else has done it, then let the compensation fall in line accordingly." (Then ask a question.)

OR

"There are some companies I wouldn't work for at double the amount I've been making, and I'm sure that there are some that I would go to work for at a lesser figure." (Then ask a question.)

OR

"It's not just a question of what I want but more a matter of what I'm worth to you. I think I'll leave that open to your own sense of fairness." (Then ask a question.)

OR

"I imagine you have a range in mind and I'm certainly open to negotiation. I think after we've discussed your needs a little bit more and compare my experience in solving similar problems, we'll both have a better idea of where we should begin." (Then ask a question).

_____

_____

_____

_____

_____

_____

_____

_____

_____

_____

_____

_____

_____

_____

_____

_____

It's very important to recognize that any and all of your responses must be in your own words. These examples may or may not "fit" your particular personality, but the basics are pretty much the same for everyone.

FUEL THE FIRE!
After you get the job offer, push your upper hand for all it's worth. This is not the time to let up. In fact, it is time to get really tough. The interviewer may not be pleased if he ends up paying you more than he had expected to, but after you start working for his company, you will get along much better with him, since you have already gained his respect for you as a good negotiator and closer.

Take a Close Look

Before accepting any new position, always make sure that the company in question is creditworthy. Make an honest assessment of its capacity to stay in business and to compensate you adequately on a continuing basis. Incidentally, if you find it easy to wrap up a high-compensation package, you had better take an even closer look at the credit-worthiness of the company involved. And don't let your emotions rationalize you into a bad situation.

A PENNY FOR YOUR THOUGHTS
Regardless of your talents, most prospective employers will attempt to evaluate your potential worth to them in terms of your present or past earnings. If you have been making $17,000 a year, it is highly unlikely that you will be considered for a $27,000 position. If, on the other hand, you have been making $23,000, a $4,000 increase to $27,000 would not seem out of line. This antiquated and un-

WHY SHOULD I HIRE YOU? 137

reasonable barometer for measuring financial packages is a major weakness of our commercial system. Most companies use it, and so do a great number of *individuals* who unrealistically categorize their own potential dollar value. These people usually fail to negotiate and end up accepting low salaries. To secure a substantial salary increase you must either seek out companies that don't use your salary history as a guide or else learn how to handle the ones that do. You could lie, of course, but before you exaggerate your present or past earnings, bear in mind that it is easy for a company to check on you. Don't gamble unless you can afford to lose. For obvious reasons, I don't recommend or condone lying to a prospective employer.

Hopefully, of course, you will have obtained a job offer *before* you start negotiating salary. Close the offer first and *then* negotiate compensation, or, in any event, delay talk of salary as long as possible. Leave fringe benefits until last. Stock options and profit-sharing programs should be negotiated separately *after* you have reached a firm agreement on the base compensation figure. Never make irrevocable demands. Always leave yourself at least one or two options. (It also works the other way around. Any person who says to his boss, "Unless you can meet my demands I'll be forced to quit" is asking to be fired.)

VELVET HAMMER

If hiring is emotional, then salary negotiating is hysterical. Define your opponent's weak spots during your early interviews and then hammer away at them when you negotiate salary. Since he is not a professional interviewer, he almost certainly will expose his soft underside to you, and when you spot it, move quickly before he has an opportunity to recover.

Here are some suggested ways to handle the matter:

"Look Mel, I'm not asking for any guarantees, and you're not offering any. We've arranged a good marriage, and I think we both realize it. The $4,000 standing in our way is vitally important to me and to my family. Mostly, though, it would be your vote of confidence. We both know what happens when a person doesn't measure up to his boss's expectations, and you're obviously convinced I'll perform or you wouldn't have hired me. So please treat me as a member of the team and not as an outsider. Now I'd still like to plan on starting on the fifteenth if you have no objection." (If he doesn't object you're in!)

OR

"Look Mel, if you wanted a $1.98 job done you'd be talking to a $1.98 person. You're good for me and I'm good for you and we both know it. We're talking about $4,000, which the company can readily afford and which I can't. Now if you have no objections, I'd still like to plan on the fifteenth as a starting date." (If this language seems a bit stout, let me remind you that you are talking about *your* money, *your* tomorrows, and *your* family, and your new company will never permit you to forget your starting salary. Chances are it will be used as a means of measurement for any future salary increases.)

"Mel, please don't compare my salary to that of the last person who filled this spot. If he had been the right person for the job, he'd still be here. We're talking about $4,000, which is probably less important to you than it is to me. Frankly, I would be flabbergasted if you were more concerned with price than with quality. (Pause) When I leave here the first thing I'll do is submit my resignation to my present company, so if you have no objections, let's plan on the fifteenth as a starting date." (Then shut your mouth, shake hands, and leave!)

Notice that the interviewer has not been forced to say yes or no to the question of the additional $4,000. The interviewee has simply forced him to assume that the higher salary is an accepted fact and that the only area of question is the starting date. (Re-read this paragraph at least ten thousand times.)

The bigger the starting salary the better. But you must also consider prospects for your financial future. A company that has a very structured pay scale probably will also hand out increases in a standardized manner. If you foresee these conditions in a particular company, don't go near it unless you are willing to accept the amount they offer. And if you are already in such a situation, it might be re-assessment time.

IT'S ONLY MONEY

Don't accept a job offer too quickly. Try for several good offers before you make any final decisions—always preserve your freedom of choice. Don't be forced by a lack of alternatives to accept a position you don't really want. Even when you have several options, there is no guarantee that the position you accept will turn out to be precisely what you had hoped for. But certainly the likelihood is greater. Job seekers too often relax their efforts when they are close to one job offer and then completely stop negotiating with other firms the moment the first offer is firm. Don't wait too long to make a decision, but don't go so fast that you end up taking the wrong position.

You Can Take It With You

Let your prospective employer make the first financial commitment. Who knows? He may

ILLUSTRATION 21

be thinking of a figure substantially higher than the one you had in mind. And never assume that the salary range and fringes set forth by your interviewer are rigid and inflexible. Not all positions offer a wide range of starting salaries, of course, but when they do, don't settle for the lower end.

And do your homework before entering into salary negotiations. Prepare a checklist that includes salary range, stock options, bonuses, incentives, insurance, automobiles, expense accounts, future increases, increase reviews, and future promotions. List them in order of importance starting with salary, and leave the standardized items, such as group insurance, until last. Then assign a dollar value to each

_____
_____
_____
_____
_____
_____
_____
_____
_____
_____
_____
_____
_____
_____
_____
_____
_____
_____

item. Your checklist will help bring things into focus so that you can negotiate each item in a logical sequence.

Two Separate Laundry Lists

Compensation objectives, like other goals, also come in two basic colors: short term and long term.

SHORT-TERM OBJECTIVES
1. Base salary
2. Commission
3. Expense account
4. Overrides
5. Relocation expenses
6. Company car

LONG-TERM OBJECTIVES
1. Future salary reviews
2. Stock options (and other forms of future ownership)
3. Profit-sharing
4. Position promotions
5. Pension and retirement plans
6. Life, accident, and medical insurance
7. Bonuses based on performance
8. Company-paid travel
9. Vacations
10. Sick leave
11. Company discounts (on its product or service)
12. Credit union or other sources of saving and borrowing
13. Company-paid education
14. Experience gained that can later be converted to earnings

15. Exposure that can later be converted to earnings
16. Company-paid social and recreational advantages

In general, you should settle the short-term items before worrying too much about the long-term items. And be sure to tie the whole thing in with your original short-term and long-term job objectives.

DEFINING PAYDAY

Short-Term Compensation Areas

1. *Base Salary.*   This is the starting point from which you can do a lot of financial somersaults. This is the figure you talk about (or are embarrassed to talk about) when an interviewer asks you how much you were making. This is the magic dish of digits that will dictate your standard of living and your future level and rate of advancement. So go after it as though it were your last chance. It may very well be just that. And nothing should be accepted in lieu of base salary. Not equity ownership, not any promise of something that will happen tomorrow. Nothing at all, just money.
2. *Commission.*   Some jobs are based entirely on commission, of course, while others offer no commission at all. If the amount of money you are to receive from commissions depends on the performance of people over whom you have no control or influence, it probably won't mean much. Commission income should be tied

———————————————

———————————————

———————————————

———————————————

———————————————

———————————————

———————————————

———————————————

———————————————

———————————————

———————————————

———————————————

———————————————

———————————————

———————————————

———————————————

———————————————

———————————————

directly to *your* performance. Not that of third parties.

3. *Expense Account.* Any profit you make on an expense account is dishonest. It's criminal, and you are guilty of cheating your company, your country, and your fellow taxpayers. Yet almost everyone who has an expense account makes money on it. Only you can measure the personal value of your expense account. *Just remember* that if you abuse it you might later find out that it proved to be your downfall.

4. *Override.* This is a different kind of commission, but it is usually associated with the performance of employees under your control and leadership. If you have good people and know what to do with them, overrides can represent a substantial amount of money. After arriving at a fair and equitable formula with your company, the rest is up to you. Don't hesitate to negotiate an override just as you would negotiate salary. Because the man you replaced might have received two percent doesn't mean the company can't pay you three percent.

5. *Relocation Expenses.* It is becoming more and more common for companies to pay these expenses. It is also fairly common for a company to buy a new employee's old house or to reimburse him for a loss suffered in the sale necessary in relocating. At the higher job levels, companies have even co-signed mortgage notes to help a new employee acquire a more attractive interest rate. Be sure to check with your accountant or tax attorney regarding such reimbursements to get a clear

understanding of the possible tax consequences of such transactions.

6. *Company Car.*   Most employees and companies alike consider a car and its operating expenses to be a real plus factor. But you should apply the same guidelines you use with the expense account.

Now, The Long-Term Money Talk

1. *Future Salary Reviews.*   Before finally negotiating your base salary, be sure to familiarize yourself with the company's salary-review habits. Sometimes they aren't as standardized as the interviewer might lead you to believe, so don't assume that you have to stand in line with everyone else. Try to shorten the time for reviews by negotiation, and plant your seeds early for future salary negotiating. If your starting salary is $2,000 less than you think it ought to be, and could be, then try to make it up in the first salary review, perhaps even on a retroactive basis. You might try this tack:

> *"All right, Mel, we're stalemated because of a $2,000 discrepancy in salary. I'll make the concession and start Monday morning, because I have faith in my ability. However, let's reduce my review period from six months to two months and agree that whatever increase you feel my performance deserves be made retroactive to my starting date. Shall we shake on it?" (Strange thing about*

_____

_____

_____

_____

_____

_____

_____

_____

_____

_____

_____

_____

_____

_____

_____

_____

_____

_____

_____

shaking hands. It is universally accepted as the final seal to a deal and is one of the most potent and effective tools available in closing. Yet few people have the crust to do it. Test it sometime on a trial close and you might be surprised. When you get an opening, just stand up abruptly, thrust your hand out so that it can't be avoided, and say, "Mel, we've talked long enough, I'll start on the fifteenth"—and you probably will).

2. *Stock options* (and other forms of future ownership). No one gets rich working for "ordinary" income (the Internal Revenue Service sees to that). So we all look for tax advantages, and ways to carry out our long-term financial planning. Stock options can provide an excellent opportunity for long-term financial gain, but you should use some very basic considerations to measure their value:

  - The ability of the stock to compete in the public marketplace.
  - The ability of the company to cause the stock to appreciate.
  - Your ability to legally influence the value of the stock.
  - The time frame in which you may exercise your options.
  - Your financial ability to exercise your options within the time frame.

Stock options, like many other "extras" should not be accepted *in lieu of* salary but rather *in addition to* it.

3. *Profit sharing.* Fine, if there is profit to

share. It's that simple and probably involves little negotiating.

4. *Position promotions.*   Don't be put in a position where you have to wait for your boss to die in order to get a better job within your company. The temptation to you is too great and the penalties, if convicted, are stiff. At the outset, try to negotiate some latitude so that you can *create* a new position later on if need be. And remember too that the odds are pretty good that you will continue to change jobs (though not necessarily companies). The average American male under the age of thirty-five changes jobs about once every eighteen months, and those over thirty-five change about once every three years. So, as soon as you start one job, immediately begin working toward the next.

After you learn something about the promotion habits and policies of a target company, your questioning should be very direct. Start by asking the interviewer about himself. How long has he worked for the firm and what has been his promotion experience? How about other members of the staff? Find out which positions within the company are occupied by people who have held the jobs for a long time without being promoted, and why. Try to determine *why* some have progressed rapidly with the company and others have not. The more you find out now, the better your chances for doing the right things later—after you start.

During final negotiations with your target company, you can usually do a lot toward clearing a path for the future. Be

_____

_____

_____

_____

_____

_____

_____

_____

_____

_____

_____

_____

_____

_____

_____

_____

_____

sure to emphasize your interest in growth; make the interviewer spell it out for you. Ask about the company policy on changing departments and crossing corporate lines. Sometimes you can even get the interviewer to commit himself to giving you a promotion based on certain conditions—perhaps when you pass your bar exam or complete your M.B.A. or achieve a certain profit level. Ask such questions as "At what future point do you feel this particular function will have to be split off and will become a department of its own?" Don't tie your future promotions to the calendar or to the actions of someone else (when old Fred retires). *Maintain control.*

5. *Pension and retirement plans.*   There is usually little to negotiate in this area, but be sure to get the details. Company participation and benefits can vary widely, depending on your position level. Such plans are ordinarily quite inflexible, but you may find a little room for negotiation.

6. *Life, disability, and medical insurance.* There is little room to negotiate here except at the very highest levels, but there's no harm in collecting the details. Find out if the coverages can continue after your employment with the company terminates. Ask about the cash-value accumulation (if any) of the life-insurance coverage and who actually owns the policy. Find out if "term" insurance can later be converted to "ordinary life." Get the details of medical and disability insurance, ask about the extent of coverage for your dependents—and find out who pays for what. Sometimes you will have to gather

the details from the personnel department, since the interviewer might not be knowledgeable in the matter. You can usually do nothing about increasing established insurance coverages, but by all means find out about them.

7. *Bonuses based on performance.*   As with commissions and overrides, try to make certain that bonuses will be contingent on *your* performance, not on the performance of those over whom you have no control. And just because a firm has never paid such cash rewards doesn't mean they can't or won't. A well-thought-out plan that puts the proper incentive on both ends can sometimes work wonders. If a company refuses to consider a bonus arrangement, you can sometimes lay the groundwork so that in the future you can bring the matter up again.

8. *Company-paid travel.*   Go easy in this department. Although many companies encourage you to take your spouse along, this can be a very sensitive subject. Don't forget that any benefits you receive must *always* be in the best interest of the company (at least in the eyes of the interviewer).

9. *Vacations.*   If you are interviewing at a lower level, you will probably want to simply get the details. If, however, you are interviewing at a level where vacations are variable or perhaps left pretty much up to your discretion, don't even bring the matter up. Leave your vacation plans out of your negotiations.

10. *Sick leave.*   Don't even talk about it unless to mention in passing, "In my adult life I've never missed even one day

———————————————
———————————————
———————————————
———————————————
———————————————
———————————————
———————————————
———————————————
———————————————
———————————————
———————————————
———————————————
———————————————
———————————————
———————————————
———————————————
———————————————

on the job because of illness." Sometimes you can accumulate unused sick leave and convert it to time off or even to cash, but this is not a matter to be pursued during your salary negotiations.

11. *Company discounts.* This factor will probably be of little concern to you unless your company happens to be in the retail business. Most companies that offer employee discounts do so on an established schedule.

12. *Credit unions and other sources of saving and borrowing.* This is an increasingly significant company tool for attracting good employees, but it is quite standardized in its application. No room for negotiation.

13. *Company-paid education.* This can usually best be negotiated *after* you start work, unless it seems to be a significant factor to the interviewer in the beginning. If you are expected to eventually complete a degree or to go back to school you will want to find out about company policy in such matters. If no policy has been established you might try, "I'll be happy to spend the time and effort, Mel, and I assume that the company wouldn't mind the expense." It is also a good idea to find out the company's attitude concerning "outside" seminars, workshops, conventions, association meetings, and the like. These costs are ordinarily absorbed by the company, but some companies are much more aggressive in this area than others. Generally speaking, this matter requires little negotiation.

14. *Experience gained that can later be converted to earnings.* Don't overlook

this one. Remember your unceasing
effort to become more valuable to
employers. If you can establish an
understanding right from the start that
you will be permitted to wear many
different hats (from time to time), you
will gain immeasurable advantages. If
you are in engineering, for example, you
might be in a position to gain experience
in marketing and accounting. If you are
in accounting, obtain license to become
involved in personnel. Although you
won't be able to negotiate the specifics of
this issue before you actually start
working, you can certainly reach an
early understanding with the
interviewer to ensure you will not
become permanently pigeonholed.
Always keep yourself in a position of
maximum exposure to guarantee
continued job growth.

15. *Exposure that can later be converted to
earnings.* You must first gain *exposure*
so that you can then develop *opportunity.*
(Remember?) Anytime you can sit in,
even as an observer, on a staff meeting or
other management functions, do so. If
you can represent the company in civic
groups, trade associations, or the
Chamber of Commerce, do so. You need
constant exposure to the "outside world,"
to your higher-ups, and to your company's
competitors. Your attitude, plus the
groundwork you lay during your initial
negotiations, can make a big difference
down the road, so be sure to treat the
subject with the emphasis it deserves.
Continued *exposure* is vital to your
continued *opportunity.*

16. *Company-paid social and recreational*

advantages. Although this is probably not an appropriate subject for negotiation, it should be noted that some firms are very big on extracurricular activities—those that are will let you know about it in a hurry.

17. *Nurseries and Day Care Centers* are also provided by some employers, especially the more forward-thinking firms, which are equal-rights oriented.

SAY IT AGAIN, SAM

Let's go back now to the base salary and cover some details. In establishing your starting salary a number of considerations can get into the act:

1. Your salary history, particularly what you earned in your last (or present) job.
2. The salary arbitrarily established by the company for the job in question.
3. Your personal financial requirements.
4. The amount that the company can afford to pay.
5. The amount established by comparable positions either within the company or within competing companies.
6. The amount earned by the person you are replacing.
7. The present need to fill the position—and the company's deadline.
8. The amount allocated by the company budget.

There are other factors as well, but the only one that really counts is: *THE AMOUNT THAT YOU ARE ABLE TO NEGOTIATE.* And only under extremely unusual circumstances should you consider a lateral or a downward move in base salary.

If you are plagued with a history of low earnings, your work is cut out for you. Don't apologize for it. The more you talk about it, the more of a problem it can become. And don't draw attention to it by bringing it up in your interview. If you are negotiating for a salary that is substantially higher than what you have been making in the past, and the interviewer tries to bury you there, turn it into a positive. Here are some tactics you might try:

"That company doesn't have a reputation for overpaying, Mel, but the knowledge I gained there is priceless."

"You're right, Mel, I've taken it on the chin financially, but my time with that company really helped in preparing me for this step."

"It's true that I could have earned more money had I chosen different past employers, but I don't think I would be as well prepared as I now find myself."

"I suppose most of us would have enjoyed more money along the way, but the learning experience must be paid for one way or another. I'm at least happy that I didn't have to go into debt for it."

_____
_____
_____
_____
_____
_____
_____
_____
_____
_____
_____
_____
_____
_____
_____
_____
_____

OR

"I know what you mean. Can you imagine the hardships experienced by professionals such as surgeons, who must sometimes finance their entire education and early experience?"

OR

"I'm not pleased with my past earnings, but I'm proud of the qualifications I've gained through that sacrifice."

OR

"Sure, more money would have been nice, but now my philosophy of building for the future is starting to pay off."

OR

"I'm glad I didn't fall for the fast-buck approach to my career. I'm now in a position to command a very respectable income, and I don't have to back up to the pay window when I take my check."

(After your response, come right back with a question to shift the conversation and regain control of the interview.)

Sooner or later, a figure will have to be mentioned, and if the interviewer mentions a figure that is higher than you had anticipated, you have no problem. Just try for more, then close. Generally, however, the first figure you get will be less than you had hoped for.

Let's assume that you have been making $16,500 and that you have now successfully controlled three interviews with a new company and have received a job offer. Let's further assume that you feel the new job should start at $22,000, based on all of the information you have been able to gain along the way, but you are quite sure the interviewer would consider a jump of $5,500 to be excessive. (Remember that he is obligated to make the best possible deal for his company.) Your discussion might proceed in this manner:

INTERVIEWER: You've been at $16,500, Henry, and I'm willing to start you at $18,000. That's a fine increase, and I assume it's all right with you.

INTERVIEWEE: That's a good starting place, Mel, but from our past three conversations I think we're both talking about a $23,000 or $24,000 responsibility. Can you tell me why you thought it should be so much less? (He can't, of course, but he'll try.)

INTERVIEWER: Well, for one thing, you'll be starting at the same salary as the man you will replace, and he had been with us three years.

INTERVIEWEE: I've never met the man, and he probably did a good job for you at the time. I don't think, though, that you would have hired me if you weren't certain that I am exceptional. It seems to me that you can no longer afford an $18,000 man for a $25,000 job. Do you agree with that reasoning?

_____

INTERVIEWER: There's no way in the world that I could justify $25,000 for this job, Henry. What's your minimum figure?

INTERVIEWEE: If I could afford it, I'd work for you without a salary, but since I can't, I'll rely entirely upon your sense of fairness. Don't worry about your justifying the $25,000. It's up to me to justify it, and I've already committed myself to that responsibility. In terms of an investment, we're both convinced that the results will show up immediately in savings for the department, so let me suggest something. I'm willing to start at a lower figure—say $23,000 in order to get us off dead center— with a gentleman's understanding that at the end of my first ninety days, you'll take a scrutinizing look at my performance and then make an upward adjustment if you feel it's in order. You're a good negotiator, Mel, and I'm glad we're on the same team.

Now, go for the close. Stand up and extend your hand. If he takes it you've got a deal. If he doesn't, you have still gained ground. Remember, you're not trying to make him *say* "okay, we have a deal," you're only trying to avoid his objection to your proposal. If he doesn't object, you're in. Notice that the interviewee hasn't yet mentioned $22,000, the figure that he is trying for. He has left himself room for negotiation and compromise. *Be patient*. This part of your negotiating is exceedingly important, and if you have done your job right in your previous interviews with this interviewer, it's unlikely that you'll blow the whole thing during salary negotiations.

DON'T GIVE UP. ALWAYS ASK WHY:

"Why do you feel the position shouldn't start at $25,000?"

"Why do you feel I'm not worth $25,000?"

"Why do you feel you can afford an $18,000 man?"

"Why was the former man getting only $18,000 after three years?"

"Why do you feel the $25,000 would not be a good investment?"

Prepare a lot of these questions. If everything goes well, you will need them. Will he really answer these questions? You bet he will. And he'll tell you exactly what you have to know if you simply encourage him to talk. Through your questions, guide his conversation back to a closing opportunity, then trial close again—*on a minor point*. And when you sense that you are pushing him to the brink, back off a little and build again. The key word here is *patience*. Your earlier interviews set the hook in deep and solid, and now you have only to land him. You gave him the bait in your first interview; the second interview locked the hook; and now you're reeling him in. But don't jerk the line—no sudden moves or wide digressions from the ordinary. *Exercise extreme patience*. When the line gets too tight, ease up before it breaks. As long as the hook is in solid, you won't lose him. And then ease him into the boat. Be gentle but firm. Now use a minor point as a net and close—gently, firmly, decisively. Ah! That feels good!

DON'T BE EASY

If the salary for a position has already been firmly set, and there is absolutely no flexibility, you should have discovered this fact during earlier interviews. Such is not ordinarily the case, unless you go with a government or some other non-profit entity. In almost any other situation, you can *and should* negotiate. Never settle for the first figure offered, even when it is more than you had been thinking of. A word of caution, however. If you are offered an unrealistically high salary, or if the interviewer seems *too* easy, you'd better find out why. The company might be in financial trouble, or perhaps you are being hired for a very short-term assignment without even realizing it.

Here's another hypothetical salary conversation:

INTERVIEWER: What sort of salary do you require?

INTERVIEWEE: Like most others, I've set some financial goals of my own that I feel are in keeping with my value to a company. I've been interviewing in the $25,000 range, and, quite frankly, I don't think there are very many positions below that level that would offer much of a challenge to me. We haven't really covered salary yet, but I'm sure you won't treat me unfairly. What do you suggest?

INTERVIEWER: I'd set the starting salary at $18,000, and then, if it works out, you'll have plenty of room to grow. I'm a firm believer in seeing the performance first, then the salary will follow accordingly.

INTERVIEWEE: So am I, Mel, and I agree that the trust must flow in both directions. Neither of us is trying to take advantage of the other; we're just trying to agree on an amount that's fair. I'm not going to set an absolute minimum and take a chance on putting us in a deadlock. The job is far too important. I do ask, though, that you not categorize me along with the applicants you refused to hire. Even if they had been willing to start at $18,000, it really isn't relevant, since I'm the one you chose. Maybe a soft compromise between the two figures is the answer. Let's meet halfway and then take a closer look at it in three months. That way, everyone is getting fair treatment, and it still gives me something to shoot for. That reminds me, I'd like to stop in and see Mrs. McKee in Personnel. I promised her I'd fill out her personal-data form today.

—————————
—————————
—————————
—————————
—————————
—————————
—————————
—————————
—————————
—————————
—————————
—————————
—————————
—————————
—————————
—————————
—————————
—————————

(Then try to close. Stand up and seal it with a handshake. It will be tough for your man to refuse to shake your hand. But if he does, come back with a "why" question, and begin the process over again. Begin it over again as many times as necessary. And don't forget the key word—*patience*).

ONE LAST TIME: THE FINAL NEGOTIATION

The final negotiation of compensation usually deserves a separate interview, and by that time, you should have developed a good idea of the salary you will try for and the range the interviewer has in mind. If he is thinking about $18,000, and you are thinking of $22,000, do some homework before you get into the final negotiating process. Try to think of any and all reasons (or excuses) why he won't pay you $22,000, or why he wants to pay you $18,000. Don't overlook the fact that setting the salary, like agreeing to hire you in the first place, is a highly emotional process, and the interviewer may not be thinking logically at all. Perhaps the $22,000 amount is a lot more than he was making at your age, or maybe he will be embarrassed when he has to justify the amount to his boss. Perhaps your salary will be charged to his budget in such a way that it will affect his own personal income, or perhaps he made a serious blunder in the past—starting someone out at a high salary, only to learn later that he should never have hired the person at any price. No matter how ill-defined his reasons might be, you can be certain that he does have some reservations. And as meaningless as they may appear to you, they are important and real to the interviewer.

Next, mentally work out responses to every conceivable objection he might raise, but make sure that these responses are honest and direct.

Keep Your Cool

Never argue, just negotiate. Don't lose your cool. *Be patient.* And don't sound as if you are selling something. If the interviewer realizes you are selling him, he will undoubtedly back off. Make him feel he is buying, not being sold. Convince yourself that he *really* needs you and that if he agrees to hire you at the higher figure, you will be a bargain for him. Maintain this mental posture throughout your salary negotiations. Don't let him get excited or emotional. If the pressure builds too much, let a little steam out, and allow him room to breathe. Lead him. Control him, but be subtle: Let him think he's the one who is in control. When you can't quickly overcome an objection, look for a different opening by asking a question that will change the focus. If an opening doesn't immediately surface, change your tack again. You need only one good opening to close. And every time the interviewer agrees with you on a minor point, you're one step closer to reaching your final goal.

In handling any objections that may arise during negotiations try to stay away from "Yes, but." Instead, use the more positive "Yes, and" approach. Here are some examples:

INTERVIEWER: You're certainly reaching high, Henry.

_____

_____

_____

_____

_____

_____

_____

_____

_____

_____

_____

_____

_____

_____

_____

_____

INTERVIEWEE: Yes, and I don't apologize for my qualifications.

OR

INTERVIEWER: That's a lot more money than you've been making.

INTERVIEWEE: You're right, Mel, and I'm glad I started planning my career at an early age.

OR

INTERVIEWER: That's more money than we pay to other people for the same sort of position.

INTERVIEWEE: Yes, Mel, and I'm going to make sure you get more than your money's worth.

OR

INTERVIEWER: $22,000 is a lot of money.

INTERVIEWEE: Yes, and it will be one of the best investments you'll make.

OR

INTERVIEWER: That's a big jump in salary.

INTERVIEWEE: Yes, and I know we'll have a good association.

OR

INTERVIEWER: That's a lot more than I had in mind.

INTERVIEWEE: Yes, and we'll make a great team.

OR

INTERVIEWER: That's a lot more than we had budgeted for the position.

INTERVIEWEE: Yes, and I think we should go through the reasons together.

(Now come back with a well-prepared question.)

Get the idea? Don't be argumentative. Don't put the interviewer down, even though you might have many opportunities to do so. Don't damage his pride. Make it easy for him to say yes. Be gently persistent. Wear him down by overcoming his objections, then lead with a question to set up a close. Then *close on a minor point*.

Always make certain that the interviewer is interested in what you have to offer, and don't spend much time responding to his objections. If you get hung up on an objection, you will take the spotlight off the real problem of setting the compensation.

Don't be too quick and clever. You will only hurt yourself by spitting out your responses like a computerized robot in high gear. You must keep his confidence. He has already hired you, and now you are merely setting the price. So even if his objections seem unreasonable, or unimportant, treat them with respect.

Some objections might be merely contrived and not really valid. Here are some possible responses to them:

INTERVIEWER: I'll have to think it over and get back to you, but it doesn't look promising.

_____

_____

_____

_____

_____

INTERVIEWEE: I understand completely, Mel, and I know you'll be fair now that we've covered everything so thoroughly. Exactly what do you need to think about?

OR

_____

_____

_____

INTERVIEWER: That's more money than we can afford, Henry, so I think I'll just put the whole thing on a side burner for the time being.

_____

_____

_____

INTERVIEWEE: I agree, Mel. Present-day salaries and living expenses are a bitter pill for all of us. Unfortunately, your problem won't go away until you get it resolved, though. Maybe I can help if you tell me what's really bothering you.

OR

_____

_____

_____

INTERVIEWER: We're having a staff meeting Thursday, and I'd like to kick it around with a few of the others.

_____

_____

_____

INTERVIEWEE: I can well appreciate that, Mel. There's nothing wrong in being thorough, and somehow the decision invariably seems to fall back on one set of shoulders. If you can give me an idea of just what you'll be kicking around, maybe I can shed some light on the problem.

OR

INTERVIEWER: I think I'll have to just wait for awhile, and I'll let you know.

INTERVIEWEE: If waiting really solved problems for companies, I guess a lot of managers wouldn't have much to do. What are you really saying?

OR

INTERVIEWER: In all fairness I think I should talk with other candidates about the position.

INTERVIEWEE: I agree in being thorough, Mel, and I also agree with your reputation for action. Why do you want to talk with a long line of job applicants?

Don't forget to use "why" questions:

- "Why do you want to kick it around?"
- "Why do you want to wait a few days?"
- "Why do you want to put it on the side burner and for what period?"

Help the Interviewer Say Uncle

You must know the basis of an objection if you are to overcome it, so make him tell you about it. Keep hammering away. Get the objection out into the open where it can be dealt with. And then, when you have satisfied the objection, don't spend time rubbing the interviewer's nose in it. Get right on to closing. In other words, don't ask the interviewer to *openly* agree with you and to admit that he was wrong. When you embarrass or humiliate him, you're only inviting him to react emotionally and in opposition to you. Let him maintain his dignity. Don't let up and don't pity him because if you do, you will immediately lose your hold. But don't make him uncomfortable either. The scale should be balanced perfectly—with your thumb on it.

Don't try to guess what the interviewer's objection is. Get to the bottom of the matter, and discover the *real* reason. Use your persistence and patience to probe, withdraw, find the opening, and then close. And if your strategy doesn't work the first time, repeat the process. Repeat it as many times as you need to, but don't let up or give up.

You Get What You Want

Your attitude spells the difference between the low and high ends of salary negotiation. It's not good enough to *need* the higher salary; you must *want* it, and you must *want* to outnegotiate the interviewer. The interviewer may have the *need* to hire you at $18,000, but it is entirely up to you to motivate him to pay you $22,000. You must make him *want* to pay you the higher amount. If he doesn't come around, it is probably not because he couldn't or wouldn't, but because you failed to convince him that he should. And if that happens, point your finger in the right direction. These are *your* paychecks we're talking about.

Selection of the right job offer often amounts to a question of money. Here's another way of putting it. If you have a job offer from a company that you don't even want to consider, you should never have interviewed to that extent in the first place. If, then, you are selecting among three offers, they should all be desirable and within your requirements. Then the nod will ordinarily go to the offer with the most attractive short- and long-term financial advantages.

Give It the Gas

After you obtain one firm job offer, it's time to accelerate your closing efforts with other potential employers. Keep a number of balls in the air simultaneously and get as many offers as you can within the period of time available to you. Then use one as leverage against the next while you are in the process of making your selection. And make your selection knowing that you aren't being forced into a decision due to a lack of job alternatives.

VII.
FOLLOW-UP:
Room at the Top

After you have made your selection and have actually started your new position, shift your attention toward your long-term objectives and future job changes.

WHO'S ON FIRST?

Most job changes should be planned at least one year in advance. Many times, of course, the job-changer is caught unprepared due to mergers, acquisitions, management realignment, market changes, federal regulations, or economic cutbacks. Changes and advances in technology, systems, and management techniques can also take their toll. In most of these unwanted circumstances, however, it is possible to avoid a crisis. The employee who doesn't keep abreast of his industry and his company and its management is asking for problems, and sooner or later he will no doubt get his share.

Job Plotting

The old adage that a strong offense is the best defense fits perfectly in job-plotting. If you are controlled by your employer, you can expect to play the job game defensively. Chances are you will be so busy playing "stay hired" that you won't accomplish much else. If, on the other hand, *you* are calling the shots, your chances of success are increased tremend- ously. To attain your short-term and long- term goals you will have to stay in control and play offensively. This is called *career man- agement*.

Know your company inside and out. Main- tain thorough and current information con- cerning its product or service, its market, and its management. Above all, stay informed on competing companies that you might consider working for in the future. If your company is the leader in its field, stick around only long enough to make yourself extremely attractive to its competing companies—unless, of course, you are gaining everything you want within your present firm. If your company is well down the ladder in its competitive position, spend the time and effort necessary to deter- mine exactly what the *leader* is doing right, and how. In other words, gain knowledge from the leader, and market that knowledge, along with yourself, to a company that satisfies all your other criteria, but whose major growth period still lies ahead.

Keep Moving

From a production-line position to your very own fur-lined spot in the executive washroom, the basics are the same. *First create the expo- sure, and then create the opportunity*. If you are an automobile salesman, use every ounce of energy and effort to be the best. Allow yourself no more than one year in the position, and don't make excuses. Then move into sales management. If that position is not available, or cannot be created in your company, change companies. And don't forget to keep a sharp tab on your competitors along the way. More than likely you will one day be working for at least one of them. If your work is production control, build a short but attractive track record, and then move up. If this involves changing companies, then so be it. If you can, aim for management. The most rewarding and high-paying positions are in the people business, regardless of what a company does to put its money in the till.

MORE EXPOSURE

There are many ways to gain and maintain exposure. Service clubs as well as trade and professional associations offer excellent opportunities for exposure. Just make sure you are *actively* involved. Talk frequently to the people with whom your competitors deal: their bankers, attorneys, advertising agents, accountants, employees, and the people who market or use their goods or services. Attend conventions and trade shows, and subscribe to all publications that cover your field. Get acquainted with business educators who know

ILLUSTRATION 22

about your field and about your competitors. Remember again that your task is to *make yourself valuable, to create exposure, to create opportunity. And it must follow in that sequence.*

NEVER STOP INTERVIEWING

After you accept your new position, make a personal visit, if possible, to those interviewers you turned down or who turned you down. Take the time to explain your present situation, and immediately establish a foundation for a continuing relationship. It's more than merely maintaining contact. It's really a matter of extending your interviews. The fact that a particular firm didn't happen to be the right one the first time around by no means rules it out for future consideration. If you can't make personal visits, be sure to follow up with a personal letter of appreciation to the interviewer. Make him feel that he hasn't really lost, except temporarily, and that the door is still ajar, but be careful not to openly split your

loyalties, since conflicting alliances can easily backfire.

Here are some examples of effective letter techniques:

Dear Mel:

I've been with the Amayon firm for only two weeks now, and already I've been able to slay a dragon or two.

I gained a great deal of respect for you during our sessions, Mel, and I'd like nothing better than to maintain our friendship even though we are carrying different company flags. After all, keen, ethical competition is good for our industry and therefore offers you and me an important common interest.

I'll need a couple more weeks to shake most of the wrinkles out, then I'll call you for lunch.

Best personal regards,

Henry

OR

Dear Mel:

The folks here at Amayon are great to work with. They've pulled out all the stops and loaded me with responsibility just the way I like it.

I haven't forgotten your comments about the future for our industry, Mel, and I'd like very much to share some additional thoughts with you.

Why don't we plan to have lunch in a week or so? If you will forewarn your secretary, I'll call her within the next few days to set a date.

Personal regards,

Henry

OR

Dear Mel:

I can't help but feel a little like I've won the battle and lost the war. However, the people here at Amayon are terrific to me, and they have some real innovative thinkers on their staff.

The last time we talked you mentioned your concern about pending legislation that could adversely affect our industry, and now that I've had more exposure to the problem, I share your concern.

I'll call you in a couple of weeks, and let's kick it around at lunch. We both have a mutual interest in bettering our industry, and I'd like nothing better than to continue our friendship.

Best regards,

Henry

The idea, of course, is to make yourself more attractive and to keep on interviewing through exposure. A natural by-product is the building of friendships with people who have common professional or occupational interests. They become a ready and important source of information and ideas, as well as an expedient route to future job advancement. In cultivating these associations, be very careful to maintain your own professionalism. Don't divulge privileged information regarding your company, and don't criticize your company, its people, its product (or service), or its methods. Make your man aware of your loyalty to your new company, but let him *assume* that your vote would go to him if you were given a choice. And don't feel that you are exploiting or taking advantage of his friendship. After all, you have talents that he may very well be able to use at some future date.

DON'T JUST DO SOMETHING, SIT THERE

The other major area of follow-up is *internal* rather than external. This undertaking also requires tact and finesse.

For the first week or two after starting a new job, don't just do something, sit there. Get your feet firmly on the ground, and do a lot of looking and listening. Be sure you have a good feel for the entire company before you start making your move, and be especially attentive to corporate politics. Companies are made up of people, people whose attitudes and behavior are determined by their individual personalities, prejudices, friendships, loyalties, strengths, weaknesses, likes, and dislikes.

Find out who is *really* calling the shots, and don't move against the power. If the company president is little more than a figurehead, and the number two or three man is being groomed for the top job, you had better know it. And don't forget that there is a good probability that new people will eventually move into the company (as you did).

If you were really on your toes, you would have tried to get a written employment contract at the time you joined the firm. Or at least you would have formally confirmed your understanding in a letter to the person who hired you, particularly in regard to future reviews of your performance for salary increases and promotions. Enforce the terms and conditions of your employment agreement, whether it is verbal or written, and be sure you are *well*-prepared for reviews.

The Honor Roll

Few students get all As from a good school without doing extra work, and so it is with your company report card. If you get Ds and Fs, you have failed and should be fired. If you get Cs and Bs, you are probably worth keeping. If you get all As, you can write your own ticket and control your career. The "marks" you obtain, and maintain, in your job performance directly reflect the amount of "extra-credit" work you produce.

Wear Roller Skates

Don't remain in the same job too long. Once you have learned everything there is to learn in a given position and have contributed everything you have to contribute, try to expand the position into new and more responsible areas. If you can no longer grow within your company, it's probably time to move on. As a guideline, set a maximum of two years for a junior position, three years for a middle position, and four years for a top position. If you

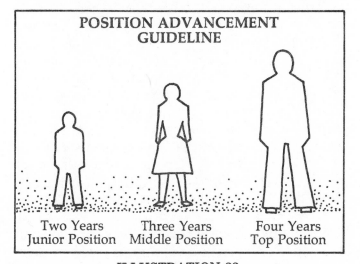

POSITION ADVANCEMENT
GUIDELINE

Two Years
Junior Position

Three Years
Middle Position

Four Years
Top Position

ILLUSTRATION 23

"If I maintain the same rate of progress during the next five years as I have during the past five years, will I continue to be satisfied with myself?"

_____
_____
_____
_____
_____
_____
_____
_____
_____
_____
_____
_____
_____
_____

have been in a top-level position for more than four years, you had better start considering another company.

Here's a question to ask yourself: "If I maintain the same rate of progress during the next five years as I have during the past five years, will I be satisfied with myself?" If your answer to this question is no then you'd better start examining the alternatives.

The late Vince Lombardi, the renowned Green Bay Packers Coach, once said, "To be a winner, a man must cultivate his talent; nurture it with dedication and determination." Fine. But how does one cultivate talent? How do you get the chance? If you are looking for a one-word answer, try exposure. Not "opportunity," but _exposure_. How many times have you heard, "If I only had the opportunity I think I could do it"? Exposure is what you are really looking for, and it's much easier to come by than opportunity. Opportunity follows exposure as surely and as regularly as night follows day.

Let's say you want to be promoted to general manager of a small company. First, you need exposure. An ideal way to get it is to create a

"To be a winner, a man must cultivate his talent; nurture it with dedication and determination."
Vince Lombardi

post for yourself as an assistant to the president, as a problem solver, or even as a short-term consultant. Once you obtain the position (exposure), you are ready to create the opportunity. Now get the facts. Identify the power structure, and don't get too close to any member of management whose position is (or may soon be) vulnerable. Get a good handle on the product or service. Evaluate the company in terms of its present and future markets. Determine what modifications, diversifications, or other actions should be implemented, and prepare a written schedule of when, how, where, and why. Examine the management. Pick out the weak and strong areas. Imagine yourself as the company's sole shareholder, its sole director, and its chief operating officer. Who goes, who stays, whose responsibilities must be changed, and how? If the company needs a financial shot in the arm, don't forget to include that factor. Also don't forget to include the competition when you are weighing present and future markets.

Once you have identified the company's problems and corrected them in your own mind, you are in a position to determine exactly how you fit into the picture. You are ready to create your own opportunity, and it is time to choose your loyalties. Now comes the most sensitive move of all. First, be sure that you have a complete breakdown of the ownership of the company. Second, try to determine the loyalties within the ownership and who is most likely to join hands with whom in the event of a major disagreement among the ownership. If the company is family-owned or controlled, be especially careful. Even though a father-in-law and son-in-law may not see eye to eye, a non-relative is still an outsider and will ordinarily be treated accordingly.

Now find out how each member of the management team first obtained a position with the company and who did the hiring. If the company's shares are widely distributed, and control is with management, you needn't be too concerned about outsiders. This information is, of course, much easier to dig out in the case of a publicly held company. Remember that management can often maintain control with only an eighteen or twenty percent position. Whenever possible, most of the information we are now talking about should be obtained *prior* to the time you accept the position.

Now determine what kind of personality, or image, the company projects. Does it have a reputation for being aggressive, forward-thinking, old-fashioned, solid and stable, a leader? A follower? A word of caution: Don't try to change things right away. This effort should be postponed until after you have achieved the necessary authority, and, even then, it should be done gradually. The personality of any operation is vital to its success and can be changed over a period of time. Ordinarily, it is a direct reflection of the ownership, and of the key management people, and can be determined within the first few minutes of exposure. If corporate advertising is inferior, the company itself will appear to be inferior. If a firm is represented in the field by a salesman who projects a poor image, then the company will gain a bad reputation. Sometimes even the slightest smudge on the corporate personality proves to be of major consequence to a company and its operations. So as you examine the personality of a company, you will actually be examining the personalities and reputation of its people. Be sure you determine which parts of the company's personality should stay and which should go. These are changes you might ultimately want to incorporate.

While you're getting your ducks lined up don't forget about politics—not corporate politics this time, but politics politics. Most business leaders are politically active, or at least politically sensitive. Additionally, the company might rely heavily on a number of political friends whose influence can have a significant effect on its operations. If your political views are not in accord with those of the management team, you might be in for some tough sledding.

After you have your game plan firmly and definitively in hand, it's time for action. Direct all your efforts toward making a hero of the person (or persons) you have decided to go with. Lay the groundwork and build a foundation. Your turn for the spotlight will come later. Your role now is not that of a lackey, but of an exceedingly vital aide. The idea is to help promote your hero's cause in any manner that will not be detrimental to the company, while giving him full credit for everything and seeking none for yourself. You are aiming for two possible objectives: 1) He will be advanced and you will be pulled along with him; or 2) Your actions will cause you to be "discovered" and possibly to be advanced without his moving. You might even replace him, a possibility you should not overlook.

From start to finish, such advances in your career should require no longer than six months or a year at the most. If your formula isn't working, it won't take long to find out, and, since time is a priceless dimension, you dare not spin your wheels. If you can't advance rapidly within your firm, change firms.

Who Me?

It's wrong to assume that success is achieved only by a few extremely fortunate individuals. Success is a process that, through proper study, concentration, and application, can be learned and adapted to your own life. If your plan isn't working, then it's either not a good one or you are applying it improperly. Act quickly and decisively to make whatever modifications you think are necessary. Remember, you are really "self-employed" and still have the total responsibility for your future.

The late Harry S. Truman once quipped, "If you can't stand the heat stay out of the kitchen." This classic statement applies perfectly to the business of career advancement. Don't expect to get something for nothing. If you aren't willing to do whatever can be done to further your career, then stay out of the kitchen. You'd only end up doing the dishes anyway.

CONTINUE TO BE SEEN

The necessity for continued exposure cannot be over emphasized. Upon beginning a new job, try to be different; be innovative, and quickly develop your own style. If you don't stand out from the crowd, no one will bother to give you a second look. Break from tradition, habit, and custom. Be better than you've ever been, and, most important, make yourself shine in contrast to your colleagues. Most company actions can be improved on, and if a chore has been handled in the same way for over a year, it is probably obsolete. Determine better ways, test them, prove them, and then incorporate them into your work and make them pay off for you and for your company.

ME TOO

In creating situations that make you visible, be careful not to get pegged as a rebel. But neither should you pattern your social and working habits in strict accordance with those of your colleagues. If you attend the same clubs, read the same books, use the same words, and perform your responsibilities in the same manner, then you can hardly expect to be treated differently than the rest of the herd. Do much more than your share. Get your name in print, take on special projects, give speeches, fight for leadership responsibilities in trade or professional associations. If you do volunteer work, be sure that it offers proper exposure and does not require an excessive amount of your time. And keep it at the adult level. Such things as the United Way or Community Chest, hospital fund-raising, Chamber of Commerce, and governing boards of educational institutions are fine. By all means don't run for political office unless you fully intend to make a career of politics. Select only those activities that provide an opportunity to work on an equal-level basis with company executives, preferably executives who are active in, or at least have an interest in, your preferred business or industry. This is not to say that you shouldn't be community-minded or help in church activities, but there are many other worthwhile endeavors. As long as you're going to give of your time and talent, get the maximum mileage for yourself.

Another important item: Seek guidance from three or four executives who are recognized as successful in your field. Their assistance and friendship can prove invaluable, and developing these connections is a relatively simple matter. First determine the groups or associations in which each executive is actively involved. Then align yourself with the same associations or interests. Newspaper libraries are loaded with information on business leaders, and it should be easy to get a fairly complete personality profile on the target executives you have in mind. You might also obtain relevant information from employees of the executive's company.

Once you have made the alignment, establish contact via telephone, correspondence, personal appointment, introduction through a third party, or a deliberate self-introduction at an association function. Then develop and maintain the contact. Such friendships take time to cultivate, so be exceedingly selective in choosing your targets. Predetermine precisely what you are most likely to gain from each association and pursue that goal. These newly acquired relationships can play a critical role in your future. But remember that the mere exploitation of another person is shallow and short-lived. You must contribute to such friendships. Assist your new friend in projects. Lighten his load, and make him look good. If you give ten percent of yourself, you will receive ninety percent in return. One of the least understood factors in human behavior is the willingness of one human being to assist another if given the opportunity. Your approach should be to offer help, not to seek help. Don't oversocialize with him, and don't use a demeaning approach, for he'll see right through you, and you will be off to a bad start. And remember that this is a personal act, not something you are doing on behalf of your company, so don't divulge private company information. Such disclosures are apt to do you a lot of harm. After you make a connection, if you find that you have misjudged and that your source is not likely to be helpful to you in your career planning, don't waste your time. Spend your efforts developing new sources.

The old saying "it's not what you know but who you know" is only partially true; in fact, it's a combination of both. Your knowledge and expertise are exceedingly important to any organization, and if you are not qualified for a particular assignment, you shouldn't commit yourself to take it on. Additionally, if you accept position handouts and advance only through personal favors, you have lost control of your own future. Your success or failure, under such conditions, depends entirely upon the ropes pulled by someone else. Remember again that your career is *your* sole responsibility, and you can't possibly be responsible for your own performance without control. Accepting a position as a personal favor from a friend could prove to be the kiss of death. If you have followed such a pattern, you'd better examine your logic. Your unconscious intention may be to fail, for this kind of hang-up is often characterized by a willingness to accept whatever is handed out to you through luck, personal favors, or fate. Here's something worth

——————————————

——————————————

——————————————

——————————————

——————————————

——————————————

——————————————

——————————————

——————————————

——————————————

——————————————

——————————————

——————————————

——————————————

——————————————

——————————————

——————————————

——————————————

repeating: 1) The best jobs don't necessarily go to the best people, but to the people who do the best job of planning for, and acquiring, positions. 2) Most people don't really know how to get better jobs and manage their careers.

KEEP GROWING

Make room in your company for yourself and your personal goals. Accepting a new job is by no means the end of something. It's only the beginning. Make yourself more and more attractive to your company—and to new companies. Keep gaining *exposure* so that you can create the *opportunity* to advance. Develop better ways of doing things. Isolate problems one at a time, and then solve them.

Keep a running, written, detailed report of your accomplishments, for this is the record you will one day play back to your present boss and probably to a future boss. It is not enough to only *feel* that you have done a great deal for your company. Be prepared to provide your next prospective boss with the full details of your accomplishments. If you keep a detailed diary you will have a heavy hammer to use in promoting your own future.

Your follow-up efforts should never cease. *Continued* effort and attention are absolutely essential if you are to *control* and *manage* your career. So keep yourself attractive to prospective employers who might potentially want to take full advantage of your transferable talents. In short, keep growing and keep going!

TIME FOR DESSERT

Try assigning a given weight, or percentage, to

the seven or eight areas of your life that receive the lion's share of your time, thought,
and effort. Individuals will differ, of course,
but your pie might be sliced something like
this:

_____

_____

_____

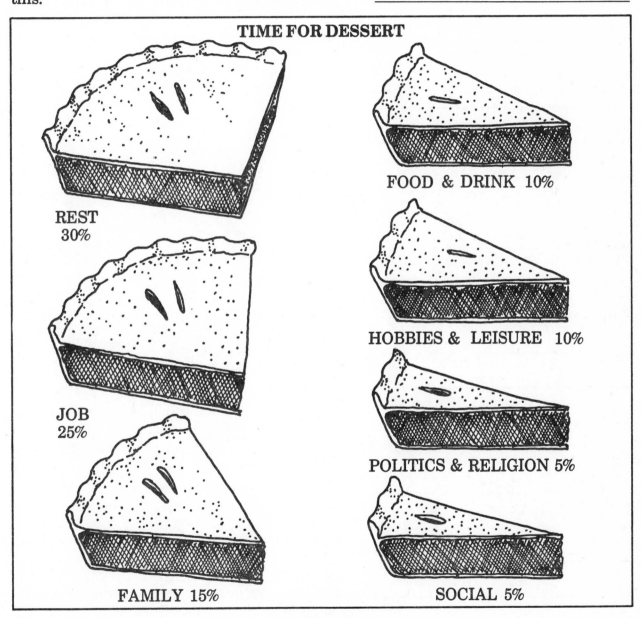

TIME FOR DESSERT

REST 30%

JOB 25%

FAMILY 15%

FOOD & DRINK 10%

HOBBIES & LEISURE 10%

POLITICS & RELIGION 5%

SOCIAL 5%

ILLUSTRATION 24

_____

_____

_____

_____

_____

_____

_____

_____

_____

_____

_____

_____

_____

_____

_____

_____

Regardless of the categories you have named and the percentage values you have assigned to each, you can bet that your job will be at or near the top. (See Illustration 24.) The "rest" portion is ordinarily the prevalent area, simply because it continues on a daily basis whereas one's weekly work schedule usually involves only five or six days. Examine your pie carefully, and you'll soon discover how important your work is in relation to the other major parts of your life.

This book has dealt mainly with the "job" portion of the pie, since that is the subject at hand. Nevertheless, it is impossible to completely separate your job from the other important areas of your life. The key is to define the job part as you would like it, fit your job to that definition, and then manage your career in such a way as to keep it within those boundaries. If your job consumes too much of your time, too much of your pie, it will infringe on the other important areas of your life. If your work takes too little of your time, thought, and effort, your life will tend to be out of balance in the other direction. If you can deal successfully with your career, then every other area of your life will have a *much* greater chance of staying within their prescribed boundaries thus providing you with a fuller and more complete living experience.

Because your job demands so much of your time, it must be taken seriously and given top priority in terms of your attention. Your job provides you with income and the basic necessities of life—shelter, food, clothing, education, and the like. Your job also provides an outlet for your talents and energies. And, to a large extent, your job determines your life

ILLUSTRATION 25

style your friends, your interests. Almost everything in your life is influenced *substantially* by your work. Most important, your job offers—or should offer—the hope for tomorrow. Without that hope, without a feeling or accomplishment, without the personal joy that welds together an individual and a company, you will be little more than a shell. No human being can make a full and rewarding contribution to himself, his family, or his fellow human beings without the *right* job.

Why, then, are most people content to remain day after day, year after year, in a dead-end position? And why is it that such a small handful of people are willing to spend the time, effort, and money to really manage their careers? Any reason you can think of is only an excuse—excuses that, for the most part, are fertilized and reinforced by needless fears and anxieties.

IT'S LATER THAN YOU THINK

One thing is certain. Almost every working person is in need of a job change, yet almost no one knows how to go about turning dreams into reality. Consequently, most people do little or nothing about seeking out a new position until they are literally forced to do so. And then it is sometimes too late. The time to act is now. Look around you. The people who actively and seriously *manage* their careers are rare. The total number of people who comprise your competition is staggering; yet the job market is wide open. Many jobs are yours for the taking—if only you are willing to put into practice the *slight advantage* that this book offers.

The Three Magic Words

Hang on to these three words, for they are the keys to successful career management:

- EXPOSURE
- OPPORTUNITY
- CLOSE

If your stay here on earth is to be everything that it should be and can be, you will have to *manage* your career. You alone must take full responsibility for its success or failure. You must keep asking yourself:

"Where have I been?"
"Where am I now?"
"Where am I going?"

And after you answer, do everything within your power to get where you are going, then keep going.

APPENDICES

_____
_____
_____
_____
_____
_____
_____
_____
_____
_____
_____
_____
_____
_____
_____
_____

APPENDIX A: WHY SHOULD I HIRE YOU?

Be prepared *in advance* to answer any and all questions that may arise during an interview. Think out your responses and *put them into writing*, using the following list as a starter.

1. Tell me about yourself.
2. What sort of job would you *really* like?
3. How can you justify our hiring you?
4. Are you ready for a job like this?
5. You have changed jobs frequently. Are you still uncertain of your career direction?
6. Will you relocate?
7. How soon would it be before you could make a contribution?
8. What motivates you?
9. How long would you stay with us?
10. What magazines do you read?
11. Who in history do you most admire?
12. What are your short-term goals?
13. What are your long-term goals?
14. What are you looking for in a job?
15. What can you do for us that someone else can't?
16. Do you work well under pressure?
17. What salary are you worth?
18. What are your three most important accomplishments thus far in your career?
19. What is your greatest strength? Weakness?
20. Why aren't you earning more at your age?
21. Why do you want to work for us?

22. Would you want to compete against me for my job? _____

23. Are you creative? Give an example. _____

24. Are you analytical? Give an example. _____

25. Are you a good manager? Give an example. _____

26. How would you describe your personality? _____

27. How many people have you hired? What do you look for? _____

28. Are you a leader? Give an example. _____

29. How have you helped to increase earnings for former employers? _____

30. How have you helped to reduce costs for former employers? _____

31. How do your subordinates get along with you? _____

32. What other companies are you talking to? _____

33. What other positions are you considering? _____

34. Why do you feel you have top [Management] potential? _____

35. Why did you major in [English]? _____

36. What were your extracurricular activities in school? _____

37. How did you spend your summers while in college? _____

38. Do you think your school grades reflect your true abilities? _____

39. How did you get along with your last boss? _____

40. Did you enjoy working for your last employer? Explain. _____

41. Why did you want to interview with this company? _____

42. How will your major strengths help you in this job? _____

———————————————

———————————————

———————————————

———————————————

———————————————

———————————————

———————————————

———————————————

———————————————

———————————————

———————————————

———————————————

———————————————

———————————————

———————————————

———————————————

———————————————

———————————————

43. In what way do you feel you can make the biggest contribution to this firm?

44. What sports do you enjoy?

45. What kinds of books do you read and how much time per month do you spend reading them?

46. Is your social life a busy one?

47. What kinds of people attract you?

48. What kinds of people annoy you?

49. What are your hobbies?

50. Why are you leaving your present company?

51. How did you happen to get into the field of [computers]?

52. Does your present company know you are planning to leave?

53. How much money do you need to live on?

54. Why are you interviewing with *us*?

55. How do you think you would fit in with our firm?

56. Why are you changing fields?

57. If you were starting all over again what field would you choose?

58. What direct supervisorial experience have you had?

59. Why were you divorced?

60. Does your spouse play an important role in your career?

61. What did you like best about your last (or present) job?

62. What did you like least about your last (or present) job?

63. What outside income do you have?

64. How much do you know about our company?

65. Is your present (or past) income

commensurate with your abilities? _____

66. Have you ever been fired? _____

67. Have you ever gone through bankruptcy? _____

68. What are your general feelings about interviewing? _____

69. Why have you been unemployed for so long? _____

70. Have you ever considered self-employment? If so, what would you do? _____

71. Why were you not successful in your own business? _____

72. How much do you want to make in five years? Ten years? _____

73. What are your thoughts regarding promotion? _____

74. Do you prefer working with others or working independently? _____

75. How would you describe the "ideal" boss? _____

76. Do you have a savings plan? _____

77. Are your debts current? _____

78. Do you live within your means? _____

79. Are you active in any outside groups or organizations? _____

80. How many hours per week do you think a person should spend on his job? _____

81. How do you define cooperation? _____

82. What do you do for exercise? _____

83. Are you a drinker? _____

84. What are the disadvantages of your chosen field? _____

85. How do you spend your spare time? _____

86. At what time do you usually get up in the morning? _____

87. What travel experience have you had? _____

88. How do you feel about vacations? _____

_____

_____

_____

_____

_____

_____

_____

_____

_____

_____

_____

_____

_____

_____

_____

_____

_____

89. What are your feelings concerning race?
90. Could you have done more in your last (or present) job?
91. What suggestions have you offered former employers that were actually adopted?
92. What are your travel limitations?
93. Why didn't you finish college? Do you have any plans to complete your formal education?
94. Do you consider yourself successful?
95. What is the most difficult assignment you have tackled?
96. What is the most rewarding assignment you have completed?
97. Are you innovative? Explain.
98. How do people criticize you?
99. How do you criticize others?
100. How would this job compare with your last (or present) job?
101. Have you ever considered running for public office? Explain.
102. Are you eager to please?
103. Are you active with your children?
104. How do you spend your weekends?
105. How do you feel about profit?
106. Are you considered by friends to be ambitious? Explain.
107. How would your spouse feel about your working for this company?
108. Is your spouse employed?
109. How do you feel about stock options?
110. Are you a motivator of people? Explain.
111. Do you ever get angry? Explain.
112. Are you tough to please? Explain.
113. Do you consider yourself a competitive person? Explain.

114. What would you do to improve our firm? And how?

_____

115. Have you ever attended night school while holding down a full-time job?

_____

116. How do you feel about an employee suing for injuries sustained while working?

_____

117. Does it bother you to fire someone? Explain.

_____

These questions are designed to force you to talk, and the interviewer will be strongly influenced, either negatively or positively, by your responses. The wording of each question will vary widely, but all of the probing can be summarized in one simple question:

"Why should I hire you?"

And if you can't handle the questions listed above, you won't be able to handle the biggie: "Why should I hire you?"

APPENDIX B: INTERVIEWING DO'S

1. Control the interview (satisfy an objection, then come back with a well-prepared question).
2. Maintain good poise, body language, and eye contact.
3. Limit the time (not over forty-five minutes for a first interview).
4. Talk profit, savings, and growth.
5. Close on a *minor* point.
6. Seek out the real meaning behind the interviewer's objections (in order to overcome them).
7. Take the time to complete your homework *before* the first interview.
8. Dress the part (Monday best).
9. Be attentive and alert.
10. *Ask for the job.*
11. Set a definite appointment for the next interview (or ask for leads if you bomb out).
12. Relax and keep your cool.
13. Avoid controversy.
14. Talk in positive terms.
15. Look for closing signals.
16. Be sure to learn all you can about the interviewer's (company's) problems.
17. Look at yourself through the eyes of the interviewer.
18. Probe for objections if the interviewer doesn't offer any.

APPENDIX C: INTERVIEWING DON'TS

1. Don't complain about anything. Not the weather, not your industry, not your former employer, and not your personal problems.
2. Don't take notes (until after the interview).
3. Don't think ahead of the conversation.
4. Don't talk money, if you can avoid it, until *after* you receive at least a tentative job offer.
5. Don't flirt or get personal with anyone in the company. (The interviewer probably knows his secretary a lot better than you think he does. You can also bet that she will pass along some sort of an opinion about you to her boss. And that opinion may be crucial. If she doesn't like your personality you could be in trouble.)
6. Don't try to sell an idea—sell yourself.
7. Don't be a name dropper.
8. Don't be cute.
9. Don't act as if you know more than the interviewer.
10. Don't interrupt.
11. Don't try to close without a closing signal.
12. Don't try to close on a *major* point.
13. Don't be too quick to give an obvious answer (think it out).
14. Don't ask multiple questions.
15. Don't ask lengthy questions.
16. Don't talk like an Indian if you're being interviewed by a chief.
17. Don't be late.
18. Don't fill out application forms unless

_____

_____

_____

_____

_____

_____

_____

_____

_____

_____

_____

_____

_____

_____

_____

_____

_____

_____

absolutely mandatory (at least not until after you get the job).

19. Don't allow yourself to be put in a position of physical disadvantage.

20. Don't talk about yourself for more than sixty seconds at one time.

21. Don't be vague.

22. Don't allow your resume to speak for you.

23. Don't permit your resume to get to an interview before you, if you can avoid it.

24. Don't interview with anyone who doesn't have the authority to hire you.

25. Don't belabor negatives.

26. Don't try to close with a question that can be answered with yes or no.

27. Don't permit yourself to be interviewed by telephone.

APPENDIX D: SAMPLE QUESTIONS FOR USE BY INTERVIEWEES DURING AN INTERVIEW

1. "Tell me, Mr. Thompson, what do you see ahead for your company in the next (five) years?"

2. "Exactly what sort of a person are you looking for to fill this job?"

3. "According to the newspaper, you plan to open a new facility in Dayton. Can you tell me a little bit about it?"

4. "How do you think the (steel) shortage will affect your operations?"

5. "What efforts are now being made to improve your (receivables) problem?"

6. "What are your plans for expanding the (sales) department?"

7. "What role do you intend for your company to fill in (civic affairs) in five years? Ten years?

8. "What plans do you have for controlling your inventory?"

9. "How do you rate your competition?"

10. "What kind of people do you usually look for?"

11. "Can you tell me a little about your own experience with the company?"

12. "What do you consider to be your firm's three most important assets? And in what order?"

13. "How do you feel your company could better serve our community?"

14. "How do you feel about promotions from within?"

_____

_____

_____

_____

_____

_____

_____

_____

_____

_____

_____

_____

_____

_____

_____

_____

15. "How did you happen to join this company?"
16. "What do you see in the future for this industry?"
17. "What have you done to find someone for this position?"
18. "What percentage of your business is tied to government spending?"
19. "What sort of personnel turnover have you experienced in your department?"

Questions of this type are designed to force the interviewer to talk about himself and his company. They help you to control the interview and gain information. Carefully prepare at least six such questions *before* an interview, and be sure to tailor them to fit each interview situation you encounter.

APPENDIX E: FORMS AND WORKSHEETS

Age	Goals	Company Profile

LONG TERM GOALS SAMPLE

SELF EVALUATION SAMPLE	
Positives (Sell this column)	**Negatives** (Neutralize this column)

About the Author

Melvin R. Thompson is a foremost authority in career management, and has established a wide reputation for his unusual approaches to getting the *right* people and the *right* jobs together. His years in the career business encompass all levels of employment, and his directness in this book is a reflection of his background. As head of a most aggressive West Coast-based career-management firm, he has left no room for excuse.

Mr. Thompson has, himself, been successful in three separate careers: mortgage banking, health-care facilities, and career management.

His uncommon approach to career problems is reflected in this book, and his no-nonsense style makes for very interesting and profitable reading.